THE SCOTTISH WARS
OF INDEPENDENCE
1286–1328

THE SCOTTISH WARS OF INDEPENDENCE
1286–1328

Andy MacPhee

HODDER
GIBSON
AN HACHETTE UK COMPANY

The front cover shows an illustration of the Battle of Bannockburn. The Scottish army appears over the crest of the hill and the English army flees, imagining themselves greatly outnumbered by the Scots, and thereby losing the battle. The insert image shows the statue of King Robert the Bruce that stands outside Stirling Castle.

Dedication
In memory of Hamish. He always loved reading about Bannockburn.

The Publishers would like to thank the following for permission to reproduce copyright material:

Index compiled by Indexing Specialists (UK) Ltd.

Although every effort has been made to ensure that website addresses are correct at time of going to press, Hodder Gibson cannot be held responsible for the content of any website mentioned in this book. It is sometimes possible to find a relocated web page by typing in the address of the home page for a website in the URL window of your browser.

Hachette's policy is to use papers that are natural, renewable and recyclable products and made from wood grown in sustainable forests. The logging and manufacturing processes are expected to conform to the environmental regulations of the country of origin.

Orders: please contact Bookpoint Ltd, 130 Milton Park, Abingdon, Oxon OX14 4SB. Telephone: (44) 01235 827720. Fax: (44) 01235 400454. Lines are open 9.00–5.00, Monday to Saturday, with a 24-hour message answering service. Visit our website at www. hoddereducation.co.uk. Hodder Gibson can be contacted direct on: Tel: 0141 848 1609; Fax: 0141 889 6315; email: hoddergibson@ hodder.co.uk

© Andy MacPhee 2010
First published in 2010 by
Hodder Gibson, an imprint of Hodder Education,
An Hachette UK Company,
2a Christie Street
Paisley PA1 1NB

Impression number   5 4
Year   2013

Cover photo: The Battle of Bannockburn, Jackson, Peter (1922–2003) / Private Collection / © Look and Learn / The Bridgeman Art Library; © Nigel Reed QEDimages / Alamy (insert)
Illustrations by Jeff Edwards
Typeset in Sabon 11pt/14.25pt by Pantek Arts Ltd
Printed in Dubai
A catalogue record for this title is available from the British Library

ISBN-13: 978 0340 987 575

Contents

Introduction

Who is this book for?

The books in this series are for students following the new Scottish Higher History Course. Each book in this series covers all you need to know about one of the most popular topics in Paper 2 of the newly revised Scottish Higher History course. The entire syllabus is covered so you can be sure all your needs will be met.

What is in this book?

This book is about The Scottish Wars of Independence 1286–1328. From 2011, Paper 2 of your Higher History exam is completely different from any earlier Higher History exam paper. There are five completely new Scottish-based topics. These topics are:

- The Wars of Independence 1286–1328

- The Age of the Reformation 1542–1603

- The Treaty of Union 1689–1740

- Migration and Empire 1830–1939

- The Impact of the Great War 1914–1928

Each topic is divided into six sections. Check out the Arrangements document on the SQA website at: www.sqa.org.uk. There you will find detailed descriptions of the content that is in each and every topic in Paper 2.

The first section you will see is called 'Background'. The last section is called 'Perspective'. Neither of those sections will have any questions asked about them. They are NOT examined. That leaves four main issues, and each one of those issues has a question linked to it.

Topic: The Wars of Independence 1286–1328	
Background	looks at the situation in Scotland in 1286, including the issues of royal authority and the relationship with England.
Issue 1	looks at Scotland in the period 1286–1296 and considers the succession problem and the Great Cause.
Issue 2	considers the reign of John Balliol and the influence of Edward I.
Issue 3	looks at William Wallace and the Scottish resistance against the English.
Issue 4	considers the role of Robert the Bruce; his ambitions and his success.
Perspective	considers the role that the Wars of Independence played in the development of Scottish identity.

What do I have to do to be successful?

In Paper 2, all assessments will be in the form of questions based on primary or secondary sources and in this book there is full coverage of all four types of questions you will meet. You will have five sources to use and four questions to answer.

You will have 1 hour and 25 minutes to do that. That means you will have about 20 minutes to deal with each question so your answers must be well structured and well developed. Put simply, that means you must do three things in each question:

1 You must do what you are asked to do.

2 You must refer to information in the source.

3 You must also include your own relevant recalled knowledge.

In the final chapter of this book there are not only examples of questions, but also full explanations of what makes good and not so good answers to the differing questions. Each type of question has its own particular process you must use to answer it successfully. In this section you will also find clear explanations of how marks are allocated so that your answers can be structured to gain the best possible score.

What types of questions will I be asked?

There are FOUR different types of question. Each type will be in your exam paper.

Question Type 1 is a source evaluation question worth 5 marks. It will usually be identified with a question asking, 'How useful is Source A as evidence...'

In this type of question you are being asked to judge how good the source is as a piece of historical evidence.

Question Type 2 is a comparison question worth 5 marks. You will be asked to compare two points of view overall and in detail. The question MIGHT NOT use the word 'compare' in the question.

The wording of the question could be something like 'To what extent does Source B agree with Source C about...'

Question Type 3 is a 'How far' question and is worth 10 marks. This question is to test your knowledge on one specific part of an issue, called a sub-issue. You can find all the sub-issues in the column called 'detailed descriptors' on the SQA syllabus website at: www.sqa.org.uk.

Question Type 4 is a 'How fully' question and is worth 10 marks. This question is to test your knowledge of a whole issue. Remember there are four issues in the syllabus on which you can be examined.

To summarise...

This book will help you to be successful in Paper 2 of the Scottish Higher History course. To be successful you must recognise the type of question you are being asked, follow the process for answering that type of question and also show off your own knowledge of the topic.

Beware: The four question types explained here WILL appear in the exam paper every year but will NOT appear in the same order every year. You will need to stay alert and be ready for them in any order.

The Golden Age of Scotland

The Golden Age of Scotland

The reign of Alexander III has often been described as the Golden Age of Scotland. From the fourteenth century onwards, chroniclers and historians have described the relative prosperity of the Kingdom of Scots at this time and the years of peaceful expansion of the central authority of the crown. But does this mean it was a 'Golden Age'? It may be that when compared with the upheavals of the Scottish Wars of Independence, many chroniclers in the fourteenth and fifteenth centuries were simply looking back on an easier time with longing. Regardless, Scotland in the thirteenth century was a kingdom increasing in confidence.

Alexander's reign saw a steady increase in the wool export to Flanders, in Belgium, an increase in the amount of money in circulation and, perhaps more importantly, the expansion of his kingdom. The Western expansion demonstrates the growth in both ambition and strength of the Scottish crown. Alexander III would have been keenly aware that the civil war in England gave him a free hand in his dealings with the Kings of Norway and Mann. The Scottish expansion into Skye and the western isles was serious enough to rouse the king of Norway, Haakon IV.

Haakon assembled a significant fleet for his defence of the Western Isles, but unfortunately delays meant that the Norwegian king was not ready to sail until late July 1263. Though impressive in number, Haakon's fleet required good weather and Alexander III was well aware of the perilous nature of campaigning in the west in autumn and winter. Eventually a great storm wrecked the Norwegian fleet on the beaches at Largs and a small skirmish on 1 and 2 October saw Haakon forced to withdraw from a small army of Scots. The Norwegian king ordered what was left of his fleet to

Source 1.1

The Battle of Largs in 1263

retreat to Orkney, where he died of ill health on 16 December. The Scottish king followed his success at Largs with a swift invasion of the Isle of Man the following year. In 1265, the Scots launched expeditions into Ross, Caithness and Skye, forcing the nobles to surrender to the will of the Scots king. The Treaty of Perth in 1266 saw the ownership of the Western Isles officially transferred to that of the King of Scots, a remarkable achievement for Alexander III.

Peace was made between the King of Norway and Alexander the King of Scots on these terms:

> 66 *Alexander King of the Scots should take under his rule and authority Man and all the Hebrides; and should pay from this year onwards a hundred marks of refined silver every twelve months to the King of Norway. In addition, 4000 marks of refined silver payable over the next four winters after the peace and excommunication is laid down for anyone who breaks the agreement.*
>
> From the Icelandic Annals, 1266

Since the time of David I, the royal government in Scotland had developed along a more traditional feudal line and the king's household would not have been dissimilar to that of England or France. Only the Earls, the one time Celtic Mormers, retained some aspect of their Celtic heritage, but even here their traditional authority was reduced and partially replaced by Royal Sheriffs.

Other countries around the North Sea regarded Scotland as a profitable trading partner and political ally. Ships built at Inverness were used to transport crusaders to the Holy Lands, Aberdeen was an important economic hub for the North Sea and Berwick was prosperous due to the wool industry. On the west coast burghs such as Renfrew, Glasgow and Ayr still had important links to Ireland, exporting timber, hides, wool and fish. Scottish burghs formed the economic backbone of Scotland and continued to provide significant support to the crown.

Source 1.2

Alexander III at his coronation

Thus, Scotland in the thirteenth century had much to offer, as historian G.W.S. Barrow states:

> *If there ever was a golden age in thirteenth-century Scotland, then it was in the 1260s and 1270s between the treaty of Perth and the death of Queen Margaret.*

G. W. S. Barrow, Kingship and Unity: Scotland 1000–1306, *1988*

Relationships with England prior to 1286

For the most part, the story of England and Scotland before the Scottish Wars of Independence was one of stability, trade and even friendship. Both realms shared the same island and both peoples had much in common. Yet two issues dominated the Anglo–Scottish relations in the twelfth and thirteenth centuries. These were the issues of the permanent borders between the two kingdoms and the question of overlordship.

Source 1.3

Political map of northern Britain

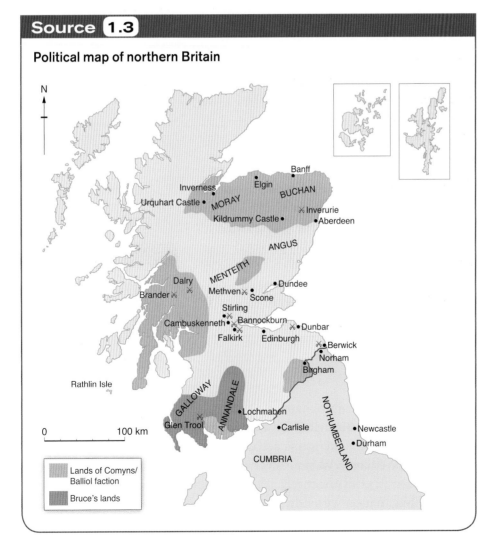

Since the time of David I, Scottish kings had long considered Northumbria and Cumbria to be within their sphere of influence. David successfully annexed the lands during the period of civil war in England. Despite reverses in fortunes, David's successors, particularly William the Lion, were quick to exploit periods of English weaknesses and used military force or political pressure to exert their claims for these lands. This instability of the northern frontier often caused a certain amount of anxiety for English monarchs. The English crown was concerned with territorial ambitions in France, and the prospect of Scottish invasions in the north was an annoyance that would weaken any French expedition. Even when the Scots formally gave up their claims to Northumbria and Cumbria in 1237 at the Treaty of York, the threat of an unstable border, or the possibility of an alliance between Scotland and France, continued to be a thorn in relations between Scotland and England.

By far the more important issue was that of overlordship. The issue was not a new one: even before the Norman conquests powerful Saxon kings had extracted admissions from other kings of Britain that they were superior in terms of social ranking. Such admissions were usually the result of military defeats, such as with Malcolm III in 1072 and, more importantly, William the Lion's humiliating agreement to the Treaty of Falaise in 1174, where he was forced to agree to English superiority.

However, by the thirteenth century the issue of Scottish sovereignty had largely been settled. Richard I had agreed to release Scotland from any oaths of homage at Canterbury in 1189, in exchange for money to finance his crusade, and Alexander II had reached a successful compromise with Henry III over the formal position of the two kingdoms at York in 1237.

The issue of Scottish sovereignty once again arose in the 1260s during the reign of Alexander III. His early years had been a troubled time for Scotland, when a series of powerful nobles and Henry III of England had taken turns in controlling the young king. However, once he assumed his personal rule of Scotland, Alexander III was clearly able to demonstrate his independent nature. A successful state visit to the court of Henry III enabled him to chastise his father-in-law for failure to make regular dowry payments. He was equally assertive when Edward I assumed the throne.

Alexander III had been emphatic in his refusal to acknowledge any homage to Edward I for his kingdom. There is an interesting account of Alexander travelling to Westminster in 1278 that demonstrates this effectively. Alexander was travelling to meet with Edward, in order to

Source **1.4**

Edward I

swear loyalty for his land in England, notably the lands known as the Honours of Huntingdon. At Westminster, Edward insisted that he should have the right to Alexander's homage for the kingdom of Scotland, should he so desire it. However, Alexander's reply was curt and to the point: 'No man has the right to homage for my kingdom for I hold it of God alone.' (From the Register of Dunfermline, which gives the Scots account of Alexander III's homage at Westminster in 1278.)

There are different surviving accounts of this meeting between the two kings but only the Scottish version contains the strong denial of English overlordship. However, if Alexander had actually given his homage to Edward for the kingdom of Scotland, any valid English documents would have been used against the Scots during the Wars of Independence.

Overall, while there were continuing issues between Scotland and England, the general relationship between both nations and their respective rulers was not in any sense aggressive. Edward I even holidayed in Scotland in 1268 and, certainly while Edward's sister Margaret was alive and married to Alexander, a close personal bond existed between the two kings.

The problem of the Scottish Church

While relationships between the English and Scottish governments were for the most part cordial prior to the death of Alexander III, the relationship between the English Church and the Scottish Church was a different matter.

Problems arose because of the lack of a Scottish Archbishop to make appeals directly to the Pope in Rome. The Archbishop of York believed that his authority should extend north and cover the Scottish bishops but the Scottish bishops disagreed.

In 1192, the Scottish bishops had successfully appealed to the Pope to prevent the Archbishop of York from affecting their independence. The Pope agreed to allow the Scottish church a special status, naming it the 'Special Daughter' of Rome. This allowed the Scottish bishops to make appeals directly to Rome without going through an English Archbishop.

Thus it was important to the Scottish bishops that the independence of the Kingdom of Scotland be maintained, as this would maintain their freedom from the authority of York. This goes a long way to explain the continued support given to the independence effort by the Scottish Church.

The death of Alexander III

The Golden Years of Alexander's reign did not last. By the mid-1280s, the deaths of his wife, son and daughter had created both personal tragedies for

the 44-year-old king and a political headache for the kingdom. Where now would Alexander find his heir? The answer was in re-marriage. In 1285 Alexander chose Yolande, the daughter of a powerful French noble family, to be his queen.

It was assumed by all that Alexander would be able to produce another heir, but he died on 19 March 1286. He had been in Edinburgh, overseeing a council of his lords, where they had been attempting to secure the release of a Scottish Baron from an English prison. After the council had been adjourned, the king decided to travel to Kinghorn, in Fife, to be with Yolande. His companions were dismayed at this suggestion, as a gale was blowing across the Firth of Forth and the weather made travelling dangerous. They did their best to dissuade the king from making the journey, but his mind was made up. When he reached the River Forth at Queensferry, the bargeman at first refused to venture across the water, and was only forced to do so when Alexander accused him of cowardice. Even when he crossed safely his officials in Inverkeithing tried to persuade him to wait until morning before advancing further into the storm. Again Alexander refused to wait and rode ahead of his bodyguards, eager to get to Kinghorn as quickly as he could. Unfortunately in the darkness and the storm, his horse stumbled and the king was thrown on the hard ground. He died from his injuries, leaving Scotland without a king.

At first it was believed that Queen Yolande was pregnant with Alexander's child. The whole of Scotland held its breath, and she was taken to Stirling Castle. However, as the weeks dragged on it became apparent that she was not pregnant and the question of a legitimate heir to the Scottish throne was now a matter for lively debate.

The impact of the death of Alexander on Scotland

The leading men of the kingdom saw the situation in Scotland as very serious. Several emergency councils were held in the immediate aftermath of Alexander's funeral. Many were eager to inform the English King Edward I; perhaps looking for his council or even protection. However, the English king's attention was, for the moment, firmly fixed on his goals in France.

When the Scottish nobles initially failed to agree on a new heir to the throne, despite meeting twice at Scone to discuss the matter, two rival noble dynasties sensed an opportunity to seize power. Robert Bruce (grandfather to the future Robert I) and John Balliol (ally of the powerful Comyn family) both saw their chance to become king. There was a genuine fear that the issue would be solved on the battlefield and many considered civil war likely. The Bruce family was led by the elderly Robert Bruce, Lord of Annandale; a powerful noble in the south west. The Balliol family was led by John Balliol, son of the wealthy French noble, Lady Dervorgilla. Both families were direct decedents of David I and, therefore, potential rival claimants to the throne.

The Maid of Norway

There was one alternative to civil war. Alexander's children had all died before him, but he had one living granddaughter: Margaret, known as the Maid of Norway. Margaret's mother, also called Margaret, had been Alexander's only daughter. She had married the King of Norway as part of the Treaty of Perth (1266), established between the two kingdoms following the Battle of Largs in 1263. Margaret had died several years previously, possibly while giving birth to her daughter. It was on this young (perhaps only 3 years of age) girl's shoulders that the hopes of many Scots now rested. If the Scots nobles could agree on her becoming the next queen then civil war could be avoided, and the Scottish royal family would not die out. Indeed, Alexander had the foresight to make his nobles promise in 1284 to accept her as heir, if he died without any other children.

Source 1.5

The Maid of Norway

> …we each and all accept the illustrious girl Margaret, daughter of our lord king's daughter Margaret of blessed memory, late queen of Norway, child of the lord Erik, illustrious king of Norway…as our lady and rightful heir of our lord king of Scotland…and against all men we shall maintain, sustain and defend her with all our strength and power.
>
> *From the Acts of Parliament of Scotland, 5 February 1284*

However, there were problems with the Maid of Norway becoming Queen of Scots. It was one thing for the nobles to agree to this as a far off contingency plan, especially when it seemed that everything was in order with the kingdom, but it was a different matter now that the day had actually arrived.

First, she was far too young to rule herself and that meant a regent would be required. A regent was a noble who would run the kingdom in the name of the king or queen until they came of age. Another possibility was a group of regents who would be named to guide Scotland until Margaret, or her future

husband, was old enough to rule. However, the question of who should become regent could easily lead to a disagreement as dangerous as who should be the next king. There were also fears for the safety of the young queen; she might be kidnapped to allow someone to gain control of the realm.

There were other issues that needed to be addressed. Monarchs at this time were expected to lead their forces into battle. However, Margaret, as a girl, could not be expected to fight for the protection of the kingdom. Many believed that a woman was incapable of running a kingdom. The obvious solution to this was to find her a suitable husband.

However, this again was a serious issue, and the Scottish nobles would have to be careful in choosing her husband. If they entrusted the kingdom to a foreign ruler it could create important issues of sovereignty in the future. If they chose a Scottish noble for her husband, this might lead to the same arguments as before and once again the threat of civil war would loom over the kingdom.

The agreement to accept Margaret as the future queen removed the immediate threat of civil war but it did not secure the long-term peace of the kingdom.

Activities

1 Draw a diagram showing the main issues of Scotland's relationship with England.

- Give yourself plenty of space. A basic, rough plan at an early stage would also be useful.

- Think about your use of colour in this diagram.

- One colour should be used to indicate developments in trade between Scotland, Europe and England.

- Use another colour for the issue of overlordship and homage.

- Different shades of the same colour should link connected points, for example, lands held by the Scots king in England etc.

- Don't forget about the issues of the Church and the borders between the two kingdoms.

- Think also of how small cartoons or diagrams could make your diagram more memorable.

OR

2 The date is November 1286. You support the adoption of the Maid of Norway as heir to the throne of Scotland.

You have been asked to write a letter to be read out at the local burgh on market day. You are asked to inspire the people who hear your letter. The Maid of Norway needs everyone's support against others who would try to seize the throne from her. In a letter of no more than 250 words, how will you convince people to support the Maid?

2 The Great Cause

The importance of the Guardians and the Community of the Realm

The Guardians

Eventually the nobles agreed to form a council to oversee the coronation of the young Queen, select her husband and settle the issue of a regent. The Guardians were chosen at the Palace of Scone in 1286. Six were chosen from different parts of Scottish society.

Two were respected bishops, Fraser of St Andrews and Robert Wishart of Glasgow. Two were barons, John Comyn of Badenoch and James the Steward; and two were Earls, Alexander Comyn, Earl of Buchan, and Duncan, Earl of Fife. The Guardians agreed that the nobility of the realm would swear an oath of fealty to the heir, Margaret the Maid of Norway. In the meantime, the Guardians would continue to rule in the name of the throne. A new seal was created to be used on royal documents. Unlike previous seals it would not bear the likeness of the king but, significantly, the royal arms and the cross of St Andrew. It may seem strange that neither Robert Bruce or John Balliol were appointed as Guardians but their potential claims to the throne may have made it politically difficult and potentially explosive to have them on a council together. However, each had their supporters among the new group.

The Bruce faction made the first move. Perhaps believing that many of the nobles would not support the idea of a young queen, Robert Bruce gathered together a small army and seized the Royal castles at Dumfries, Wigtown and Buittle. Others turned out to support Bruce, including the influential Guardian James the Steward, two other Scottish earls and the Lord of Islay. They targeted lands and allies of the Comyns and did considerable damage. There was a fear that the

Source 2.1

The seal of the Guardians of Scotland

conflict would spread beyond the south west. Yet cooler minds prevailed and the Bruces failed to win any degree of popular support outwith their own power base. The remaining Guardians had gathered together an army to oppose Bruce and for the time being the rebellion in the south west died out. However, it was a keen reminder to all of what could happen in the future.

The Guardians faced other threats to the stability of the realm. One of the Guardians, Duncan, the Earl of Fife, was accused of using his office to line his own pockets and was murdered by one of his own relatives. Fighting almost broke out in the north east, between the two Comyn Guardians and one of their rivals, the Earl of Atholl. Stability was also threatened by uprisings against Scottish rule on the Isle of Man.

Despite these problems, the fact that the Scottish nobles were able to choose six men from among themselves suggests a certain degree of political maturity and stability in Scotland. Not only did they manage to avoid civil war but they also demonstrated a significant amount of loyalty to the institution of the Scottish throne. Even without a king or queen at their head, the nobles of Scotland were able to act together for the good of their kingdom.

The Community of the Realm

Some historians believe that the ability of the church and nobility in Scotland to work together demonstrates, to some extent, the importance of the idea of the 'Community of the Realm'. This means that the powerful families in Scotland accepted that the good of the kingdom was more important than the ambitions of the individuals who made up the ruling elite. At times it has been argued that the Community of the Realm also showed a certain amount of social equality, as different parts of society, not just the ruling elite, were joined in the desire to do the best for the kingdom. However, it is unlikely that the nobles would have had any real connection with the lower classes, though the views of the church and, possibly to a lesser extent, that of the merchants in towns may well have been taken into account.

The Treaty of Birgham and the death of the Maid

Edward I, the great grand uncle of Margaret, Maid of Norway, had more than a passing interest in the affairs of Scotland. Out of respect and acknowledgment of his position, the Guardians had kept the English king fully informed of the events in Scotland, going as far as to send representatives to him in France to report the death of Alexander III.

When the proposal to marry off Margaret to Edward's young son, also Edward, was suggested it was seen as the perfect solution by both sides. It solved the potential threat of civil war in Scotland. No matter how powerful an ambitious Scottish family might be it would not choose to face the anger of Edward of England.

However, it is important to note that when negotiating the marriage treaty of Birgham in 1290 the Guardians were very careful to preserve the independence of Scotland. It was stated that both kingdoms would remain independent sovereign states; Scotland would be 'separate, free in itself and without subjection'.

The treaty was very specific about what was to remain independent.

- **Elections of Scottish churchmen were to remain free from interference from England, especially from York.**
- **Nobles of Scotland who held land from the King of Scots were to pay homage to the King of Scots for their land only; they had no obligation to pay homage to the King of England.**
- **No one accused of a crime in Scotland would have their crime tried under English law nor have their trial held outside Scotland.**
- **A new Scottish seal would be produced to be used in official documentation.**
- **No Scottish parliaments would be held outside Scotland and there would be no taxation of Scots unless for the needs of Scotland. This was a direct reference to the Scots' desire not to pay for any English wars.**

These conditions show that the Guardians were determined to maintain the independence of Scotland and that they took their responsibilities seriously. However, the Guardians could not have been happy with the situation, especially when Edward seized the Isle of Man in 1290 and demanded that the Scottish church pay taxes to England.

The death of the Maid of Norway

In the summer of 1290 most Scots were probably optimistic about the future. By October that optimism had vanished. News spread that young Margaret had died on the journey from Norway. The implications of her death were immediately obvious. Without Margaret the Treaty of Birgham was null and void and, even worse, the spectre of civil war in Scotland was once again a distinct possibility.

Confirmation of the news was slow to filter throughout Scotland, and when the Bishop of St Andrews wrote to Edward later in October he still referred to the news of Margaret's death as a rumour.

In his letter to Edward the Bishop informed the king that Robert Bruce and the Earls of Athol and Mar were already plotting and raising large bodies of soldiers and that war was likely.

In order to forestall the impending crisis the Bishop of St Andrews asked the king to come to the border in order to prevent war.

Bishop Fraser's letter clearly shows that he favoured Balliol as future king but Robert Bruce was not to be beaten. His followers were quick to raise their standards once again and he dispatched his own letter to the English king known as the 'Appeal of the Seven Earls'. The letter was simply an attack on Fraser and the Comyn/Balliol faction and an appeal for Robert Bruce's claim to be upheld.

Source 2.2

The Maid of Norway's arrival in Orkney

> " But a sad rumour reverberated among the people of that our lady was dead and because of this the King of Scotland is troubled and the community is perplexed. When the rumour was heard and published Sir Robert Bruce, who previously did not intend to come to our meeting, came with a large retinue [group of soldiers]...But the earls of Mar and Atholl are already collecting an army and some other nobles of the land have been persuaded to join their party. Because of that there is a fear of a general war and a large-scale slaughter...

Letter from William Fraser (Bishop of St Andrews) to Edward I, 1290

> " I seek urgently the help of the king of England placing the persons of the seven earls and of all the others mentioned and their followers and all their property under the special peace and protection of the king of England and of his royal crown... We appeal by the document to the assistance of the Lord Edward...for the pursuing and obtaining of our right.

Letter from Robert Bruce to Edward I, 1290

Of course, it is highly unlikely that Robert Bruce really had the support of all seven Earls of Scotland and the letter was an astute piece of propaganda. By 1291 both claimants were eagerly anticipating the support of Edward I. It was therefore no surprise that the king of England came north to the border in April 1291.

Overlordship at Norham

Norham

The Scots Guardians and claimants of the throne had travelled to Uppsetlington just north of the English border. Just across the River Tweed, Edward and a large army had established their base at Norham Castle.

The Guardians wanted Edward to come to them. They may have thought that this would show Edward that they did not accept that he had any authority over them. However, when it became clear that Edward would not move from Norham they were forced to go to him.

Edward's next move astonished the Guardians. He demanded that the Scots accept him as their feudal overlord before he would make any judgment on who would be King of Scots. The Scots were worried. Edward had a huge army with him and the Guardians may have thought this was a clear threat of military action if they did not accept Edward's demands. However, the reply of the Guardians was clever. They argued that only their king could deal with such a request and that could only happen after Edward had chosen the next King of Scotland!

Source 2.3

Norham Castle

> 66 *Sir you say you are overlord of the realm of Scotland and that the kingdom is held of you...to this statement the good people who have sent us here answer that they do not believe in the least that you would ask such an important thing if you did not consider that you had a genuine right to it. But they know nothing of this right of yours... Therefore they answer to you...that they have no power to reply to your statement, lacking a king to whom the demand can be addressed and whom would have had the power to answer it...*
>
> From the Statement by the Scots at Norham, May/June 1291

What were Edward's intentions towards Scotland?

Historians are somewhat contradictory about Edward's intentions at any specific time. It has been said that Edward was at first not too concerned about the fate of Scotland. His treatment of the Scots at Birgham would also lend some credibility to this argument. Indeed, some historians go so far as to excuse Edward's later demands for overlordship, claiming that he was overly concerned with war with France and that he was worried that Scotland might ally with France against England.

We do know that Edward had written to all English monasteries asking them to search their records and libraries for any written reference or justification for England's overlordship to Scotland, prior to the meeting at Norham. He also had his fleet on standby ready to blockade Scottish ports and was summoning fighting men from the northern counties to form an army. It was probably clear to the Guardians that his attitude to Scotland had changed with the death of the Maid of Norway, and many historians agree that this tragic incident altered Edward's intentions to his northern border. Perhaps the success of absorbing Wales into England's sphere of influence had created the belief that the same could be done with Scotland and that here was the perfect opportunity.

Most historians agree that Edward had been on friendly terms with Alexander III and simply saw his opportunity to take advantage of Scotland during its period of weakness. Even when the competitors agreed to the overlordship of Edward at Norham it was assumed that this would only be a temporary affair.

The Great Cause

The task of choosing the new king has come to be known as the Great Cause. Of the thirteen claimants, only three had a serious claim. All three were descendents of the daughters of David the Earl of Huntingdon, a

descendant of David I of Scotland. In order to ensure he would be overlord of Scotland, Edward demanded that all claimants accepted this before he would pass judgement on them. The Guardians were obviously not happy with the situation and many believed that Robert Bruce had a hand in Edward's tactics. Therefore, they stubbornly held out for as long as they could, despite constant threats of force from Edward. It was not until all the competitors capitulated, fearing they might be left out of the judgement, that they eventually consented. The agreement of the claimants is generally known as the 'Award of Norham'. By 12 June 1291 all nine of the original claimants had sworn the oath to the English king. The number of claimants eventually rose to thirteen. They all realised that this was going to be a difficult case to judge.

> **"** *To all who shall see this letter… Since we [the nine claimants] consider that we have a right within this kingdom of Scotland and are entitled to present, uphold and declare this right before the person who has most power, jurisdiction and reason to investigate our right judicially, and since the noble king Edward has proven that he has the sovereign lordship of the kingdom of Scotland and the jurisdiction to hear, try and determine our right belong to him… we of our own free will… concede and grant that we should receive justice from him as our sovereign lord…*
>
> The Award of Norham, 12 June 1291

The Award of Norham was an important acknowledgment. The claimants not only agreeed that Edward was their overlord, but that he had legal possession of the kingdom and that it was his to freely give away. This was not what the Scots had originally intended. The Guardians were furious. They had been out-smarted by Edward. Rather than being a neutral observer choosing between Bruce or Balliol, Edward was now a judge who had the right to give away Scotland. The latter made a considerable difference to the legal position of the kingdom, one that made Edward owner of Scotland.

In the end, all agreed to Edward's demands, though it was understood by the Scots that once Edward had made his choice then the oaths would revert to the new King of Scotland. This is possibly the reason that Edward took so long to make his decision. It would be easier for him to hold on to the legal position of overlord after a longer period of time. Historians, such as Michael Brown and Alan Macquarie, have pointed out that it was also going to be harder for a new Scottish king to establish his authority.

Edward's Decision

Edward announced his decision on 17 November 1292, after 13 months of political arguments and debate. In the end, John Balliol clearly had the better legal claim and was thus duly chosen to become King John of Scots. Edward's decision has been seen as controversial. Subsequent Scottish kings put forward the idea that Bruce had the better claim, and that Edward chose Balliol only because he thought he would be easier to manipulate. This was clearly not the case, despite later Scottish propaganda.

In fact, John Balliol was the last of the claimants to acknowledge Edward's overlordship. He did so only after 10 June 1291 when everyone else had already given their oath. Robert Bruce had given his much earlier. Perhaps this is a real acknowledgment of the strength of Balliol's legal position in that Bruce felt he had to win Edward's favour. It certainly diminishes the myth that Robert Bruce was the stronger man and would have stood up to Edward more than Balliol.

Was John Balliol the true king of Scots?

In strict legal terms it is clear that John Balliol had the best claim to the throne of Scotland. With Alexander III's line dead the legal team were forced to look at the earlier generation of the royal family, the offspring of William the Lion and his younger brother, David the Earl of Huntingdon. Both Bruce and Balliol were genuine descendants of David, but crucially Bruce was the son of the middle daughter of Earl David, while Balliol, though a grandson, was a descendent from the eldest daughter of Earl David. As legitimate inheritance is always passed down the eldest line until that has fully expired then it is clear that John Balliol had the stronger claim. This legal procedure in inheritance law was called 'Primogeniture'. Robert Bruce unsuccessfully argued that Primogeniture had no meaning in this situation because a kingdom was a special case. The judges decided this was not true and his application was thrown out.

Source 2.4

John Balliol and his wife Isabella de Warenne

The family tree of David I

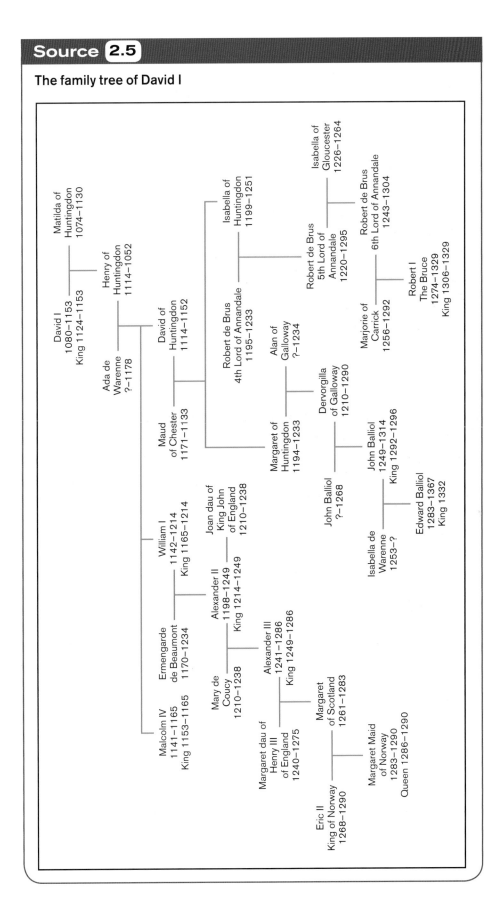

Activities

Edward I's motives are usually painted as being black, especially by Scottish writers who tend to see him as the bogey man.

1   Imagine you were asked to justify his interference in Scottish affairs in a court of law.

   • What kind of legal argument would you make in Edward's defence?

   • Outline a legal brief (an outline argument) of no more than 250 words indicating what line your defence would take.

OR

2   Teach a lesson

In groups of three or four your target is to teach a lesson to the rest of your class which is linked to the issue of whether *Balliol or Bruce* should have been named king. Your main resource for information is this textbook but you must also research, find, beg or borrow other resources to make your lesson come alive. Think of the times you have been bored just listening to someone talk. Your lesson must be different!

   • Negotiate with your teacher/tutor how long you have to prepare this lesson.

   • Your lesson should be presented in an organised, interesting, mature and informative way.

   • Planning is vital and all in your group must participate. It would be helpful to assign tasks such as a gopher to go get, a timekeeper to watch how your time is being used, a facilitator to keep things running smoothly in your group (tact and diplomacy needed here!) and a recorder to note ideas and what was suggested before you all forget.

   • Negotiate the length of your lesson with your teacher/tutor. About 5 minutes would be appropriate.

   • Your lesson must have visual material – PowerPoint or an overhead projector are possibilities.

As in any lesson there are really important things for you to decide and aim for:

   • What do you want your students to be able to do and know at the end of your lesson?

   • How will you assess the success of your lesson – in other words what will you expect to see or hear your students doing to prove your lesson has been successful?

3 The Reign of King John Balliol

King John Balliol – A bad king?

In the past arguments have been put forward that King John was only chosen because Edward I saw him as weak and easy to manipulate. These arguments are not accurate because King John had the better legal claim to the throne. His subsequent performance had little to do with the reason why he became King of Scots.

Was he a bad king? Certainly it can be said that his reign ended in failure and his refusal to return to Scotland or to carry on the fight after 1296 does not speak very highly of his abilities. It is true to say that he was placed in a difficult position by Edward I. Previous kings of England had extracted oaths of loyalty from their Scottish neighbours in the north, but this had always been more of a symbolic gesture than any real attempt to exercise authority and the Scots had more or less ignored it. King John perhaps hoped this would be the case during his reign.

Even if we ignore the issue of Edward's interference, John had many problems to overcome as King of Scots. First, he was relatively inexperienced as a politician. It is true that he was head of the powerful Balliol clan but he had never expected to be in that position. His three older brothers had all been given more instruction about ruling a major political family than John and he was personally unprepared for the task ahead. Second, Scotland had been without a king for six years. The administrative system of the Kingdom had grown weak and it would take a strong hand to make sure that royal authority was once again recognised throughout the entire Kingdom. This was particularly true in the rebellious Western Isles and among those powerful noblemen who believed that John's selection as King was the wrong choice, both legally and in the best interests of Scotland.

King John clearly had his work cut out for him. Scotland needed a period of relative calm for this new and inexperienced king to stamp his authority across the kingdom. Even the greatest of Scottish kings would have had their hands full. With hindsight, it is easy to see how King John was swamped by the events of the time. However, it is unclear if anyone else would have been able to do a better job.

Issues with Edward's overlordship

At the end of the Great Cause, when Edward finally gave his verdict to John, he reminded King John Balliol to be a fair and just king, or he would face interference from Edward. It did not take long before the ominous threat was to be realised.

The first case was brought to Edward's court only a week into King John's reign. A burgess of Berwick had a legal complaint dating from the days of the Guardians and he was still not happy with the verdict. King John had upheld the Guardians' decision, but when the burgess took his complaint to King Edward's parliament at Newcastle in 1292, the English king found in his favour. King John was ordered to change his decision. This was humiliating for the King of Scots and showed to all the true position Scotland now had with England. One was superior. The other – Scotland – was inferior.

In protest King John wrote to Edward reminding him of the clauses of the Treaty of Birgham that stated that England should not interfere in Scotland's internal affairs. In reply, Edward pointed out that Birgham was a marriage contract and without a marriage it was not worth the paper it was written on. Edward may even have ordered John to obey by using threats. John was forced to publicly recognise that the safeguards of Scotland's independence given in the Treaty of Birgham and to the Guardians before the Award of Norham were no longer enforceable. The King of England was now free from any oaths made and was able to interfere as much as he wished.

Why did John do what Edward told him to do? Remember that John was not secure in his position as King of Scots. The Bruce family were still smarting from the decision not to award the throne to them. A Scottish king who had neither the support of Edward or of his nobles might find himself removed sooner rather than later. John's strategy was to humour the English king and try to avoid any cofrontations, at least until he was in a more secure position at home.

Source 3.1

John Balliol paying homage to Edward I. Note the assembled English nobility watching from the side

For his part Edward acted rather like a bully towards the new king, treating him more like a feudal regional lord than a fellow king. For example, Edward forced John to accept a Yorkshire man, Master Thomas of Hunsingore, to be his new chancellor and John's Chamberlain was described as a Treasurer, forcing John to follow English practice rather than traditional Scottish customs.

The Macduff Case

More than any other incident, the Macduff case highlighted the weakness of King John's reign and the determination of Edward to assert his authority in Scotland. Macduff had been disinherited from his lands and had appealed to Edward in 1291 during the Great Cause. Edward had ordered Bishop Fraser to look over the case, but instead Macduff was arrested for a short time. After John's inauguration Macduff was released and once again he complained to Edward. Now Edward summoned John in September 1293 to explain his judgement of the issue. This was another humiliating demand made of King John and when he arrived at Westminster he tried to argue that Edward had no right to hear the case. However, Edward was in no mood to argue and threatened to charge John with contempt of court and confiscate important castles in Scotland. John was forced to agree to allow Edward to hear the appeal from Macduff, yet another humiliating climb down for the Scottish king. The case dragged on well into 1295 with no clear resolution.

> 66 *...the king of Scotland appeared in person before the king of England and his council in parliament at Westminster in the house of the archbishop of York and so too did Macduff and because the king of England was preoccupied with many difficult matters of business...he could not get to the trying of Macduff's complaint [and] a way was set aside for the king of Scotland to appear once again before the king of England at his parliament to be held after next Easter*

From the Record of the Court of the King's Bench, June 1294

War with France and the return of the Guardians

It was the prospect of a foreign war that caused rebellion in Scotland. In 1294, Edward was preparing to make war in France in order to pursue his ambitions there. As usual the English king summoned his feudal lords and King John was ordered to fight for Edward, in much the same way as were the great earls of England. The assumption that Scotland was to be treated

the same as the great estates of England was bad enough, but the assumption that the Scots were to fight against France, Scotland's largest trading partner, was worse. Added to this were the demands for taxes from the Scottish nobility to pay for the war. It is no wonder that the Scottish nobles were willing to revolt against Edward.

In 1295, twelve new Guardians were appointed by the community of the realm to defy King Edward. They sent envoys to the King of France and at the beginning of 1296 a treaty against Edward was agreed. It included a marriage agreement to seal the deal.

> " *In view of the actions being taken by Edward I against Philip…it was agreed that…the king of Scotland shall undertake to start and continue war on the king of England at his own cost and expense with all his power and all the power of his subjects…*
>
> *It was agreed between John Balliol and Philip the Fair, that Edward Balliol, should marry the eldest daughter of Charles, count of Valois and Anjou, Philip's brother…*
>
> From the treaty between Scotland and France at Paris, 24 February 1296

It has long been assumed that the Scottish nobility, fed up with the humiliating reign of King John, simply put their king to one side and assumed the leadership of the kingdom and of the war against Edward. However, there is no real evidence of this. It is perhaps more likely that the new king had at last found the supporters he needed to stand up to Edward and it was with the help of the Guardians that he now faced up to his responsibilities.

Why was Scotland defeated so easily in 1296?

The English king was able to defeat the Scots in a matter of a few weeks.

The invasion of Scotland in 1296 was a direct response to the refusal of the Scots to assemble for military duty and their subsequent treaty with France. However, there are indications that Edward had been planning the invasion for a lot longer than this.

Early confidence and the siege of Berwick

There was nothing wrong with Scottish morale in 1296. Berwick, the most important burgh in the kingdom, was well prepared for the conflict. Its already impressive defences were added to and more troops were rushed down from Lothian and Fife.

3

The Scottish nobles began to assemble their forces. The force was impressive by Scottish standards with 10,000 men assembled to meet the English invasion. Although most were levies, tenants called from their fields to fight as part of the obligations to their lords, there was a solid fighting core of nobles and their trained retainers. The army's confidence was high.

Source 3.2

An artist's reconstruction of Berwick castle

Unfortunately, it was confidence not based upon any real experience. In fact, the Scots had little real experience in large engagements. Simply put, confidence and large numbers of barely trained troops were not going to be enough to win the war. Despite this the Scots crossed the border and began rampaging and pillaging the northern counties of England.

> In the year of the lord 1296 on Monday [26th of March], lord John Comyn…with a large army of Scots numbering 500 knights and 40 000 infantry [a gross over-exaggeration], came from Annandale crossing the Solway at three places, burning all the neighbouring villages from Arthuret through the middle of Nicholforest to Carlisle killing or at least wounding whoever they could find, sparing neither sex, rank nor age…
>
> From the Chronicle of Walter of Guisborough, 1306–07

Edward crossed the Tweed on 12 March 1296 at the head of an impressive army. Their first obstacle was the town of Berwick. As Edward's army approached the Scottish town, the inhabitants saw for the first time the size and power of the English forces.

Edward had offered the townsfolk three days to consider the surrender, but their taunts from the town walls angered the English king and his order to attack included the instruction that none within the town should be spared.

The Reign of King John Balliol

The defenders were quickly overrun and it was not long before the few remaining defenders were forced to surrender.

The garrison appeared to have been treated well. They had fought and surrendered in line with the traditions of the chivalric code, and were allowed to go on their way once they had given their promise not to return to the conflict. However, the town's folk, who had incurred the wrath of King Edward, were not treated so well and the town was sacked by English forces.

English reports of the event suggest the invaders obeyed the rules of warfare.

Source 3.3

English soldiers at the siege of Berwick. This illustration was taken from a late medieval manuscript thus the soldiers are shown in the wrong armour

 When the city was taken they killed more than 8 000 of the enemy… The women of the city were sent away to their people after some days and went in peace.

From the Chronicle of Walter of Guisborough, 1306–07

However, other reports were more brutal.

A great quantity of booty was seized and no fewer than 15 000 of both sexes perished, some by sword, others by fire in the space of a day and a half, and the survivors, including even the little children were sent into permanent exile.

From the Chronicle of Lanercost, 1297

It would appear that there were few survivors, as Berwick had to be repopulated with English tradesmen and merchants from Northumbria.

The Battle of Dunbar

The English vanguard, under the command of the Earl Warenne of Surrey, was sent to secure Dunbar Castle. The Earl of Dunbar had already made his peace with Edward I at Berwick and had handed over the keys of the castle

Source 3.4

An artist's re-construction of Dunbar Castle

to the English king. However, his wife was a Comyn and staying true to her family loyalties she handed over the castle to the Scots while her husband was absent.

When Warenne arrived he found the castle held against him and a sizable Scottish army marching to relieve the fortress. Warenne decided to meet the Scottish force head on and, leaving a small detachment to watch the castle garrison and prevent any Scots from leaving the castle during the battle, he marched his troops to a more favourable position to await the Scots army.

The Scots for their part had established themselves upon a low hill and possibly hoped to goad the English forces to attack uphill. However, the movements of Warenne's vanguard into a battle formation were somehow mistaken by the Scots for an English retreat. Eager to prevent the enemy from escaping, the Scottish forces broke rank and rushed headlong towards the English with all attempts at tactics and cohesion forgotten in the heat of the moment. The English forces easily saw off the attack and pressed forward mopping up all resistance found.

> **"** *...soon almost at the first blows the Scots retreated and our men followed them slaying and killing for nearly seven or eight leagues almost to the forest of Selkirk.*
>
> *From the Chronicle of Walter of Guisborough, 1306–07*

The Reign of King John Balliol

The battle was a complete disaster for the Scots. Many of the Guardians and over 130 Scottish nobles were taken prisoner, meaning the majority of the leaders of the Scottish resistance to Edward's invasion were lost in a single encounter. With their loss to the Scottish cause it was inevitable that there would be a tremendous loss of enthusiasm for the war. Other commanders lost heart or simply decided that the war was effectively over before it had begun. The effect of the surrenders snowballed and gained momentum, encouraging others to follow suit.

After Dunbar there was no effective central leadership for the Scots, nor was there any stomach to carry on fighting. Things might have been different if the Scots had been encouraged by King John to carry on the fight, but without that guidance the Scots leaders fell back on the need to preserve their own lands, lives and the lives of their tenants from Edward's wrath.

In effect, the Scots were outmatched, out-thought and outmanoeuvred.

Edward's march north

The rest of the 1296 campaign was nothing short of a victory march for Edward I.

Roxburgh Castle surrendered after a very short siege, and Jedburgh and Edinburgh fell to the powerful siege engines Edward brought north with him. Worse still, Stirling Castle, the gateway to the northern half of Scotland, was abandoned by the defenders when it was reported that Edward was approaching. The keys were left with the wardens of the castles to present to the English when they arrived. By the end of July Edward had marched as far north as Elgin, accepting the surrender of all the important castles along the way.

John failed to offer any real leadership during the 1296 invasion. He did not lead the army at Dunbar and when he heard news of their defeat, he travelled north, to the relative safety of the lands of the Comyns in the north east. At Kincardine Castle he once again failed to rally the surviving nobles and without his leadership they sought terms with Edward. King John officially offered his surrender on 2 July in a letter sent to the English King.

> 66 *John by the Grace of God King of Scotland greets all who shall see or hear this letter. In view of the fact that through bad and wrong advice and our own foolishness we have in many ways gravely displeased and angered our lord Edward…therefore acting under no compulsion and of our own free will we have surrendered the land of Scotland and all its people with the homage of them all to him.*

Letter from King John to Edward I, 2 July 1296

Source 3.5

Edward's progression north in 1296

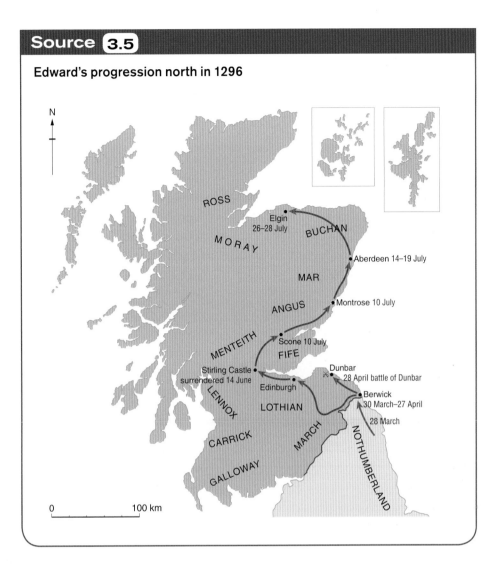

Edward accepted King John's surrender in a humiliating ceremony on 10 July 1296. King John was forced to apologise publicly to Edward and surrender his throne and the Kingdom of Scotland. The royal badge of Scotland was symbolically ripped from his surcoat by Edward himself. The act made it clear to all that John was no longer King of Scots. The incident gave John a new and more humiliating title, 'Toom Tabard' or 'Empty Coat', a title he would bear for the rest of his life.

John and his son were taken to England by ship where they spent the next three years under house arrest, being moved from castle to castle until they were eventually handed over to the Pope. King John ended his days in France, retiring to his own estates and living on a pension supplied by the French king. Despite several calls for his restoration as king he refused to return to Scotland.

The Reign of King John Balliol

Source 3.6

Toom Tabard. Note John's tabard has been torn and his sceptre broken

THE ARMIS OF THE BALLIOVN

The Ragman's Roll

Edward quickly removed any indication that Scotland was a separate country within the British Isles. All documents relating to the Scottish throne were removed and taken to London by ship, which promptly sunk; depriving historians of a wealth of information about early Scotland and Pictland. The Stone of Destiny, on which all Scottish kings had been inaugurated, was taken from Scone and transported to Westminster. In a symbolic gesture, Edward had a wooden throne made to house the stone in its seat. The Scottish Crown Jewels followed, including the important Black Rood of St Margaret. His message was clear. Edward was now the master of the future of Scotland, and that future would include England.

In late August, at Berwick, almost 1600 leading Scottish nobles and burgess swore a personal oath to King Edward. This was collectively known as the 'Ragman's Roll'. This was an unprecedented demand by Edward, and the large number of names shows how fully his domination of Scottish politics had become. Although some names occur more than once, it still represents the majority of the important figures in Scottish society.

Robert Bruce and his son, the Earl of Carrick and future King, signed the document despite having sworn loyalty to Edward as early as March. It is recorded by the chronicler John of Fordun that Robert Bruce had asked Edward for the throne of Scotland while at Berwick. Edward replied, 'Have we nothing else to do but win you kingdoms?' Edward had no intention of giving away power in Scotland, to the Bruce family or anyone else.

It has often been suggested that William Wallace's absence from the Ragman's Roll was a sign of his defiance of the English king and his intention to carry on the fight in the name of King John. However, it is more likely that he was not considered important enough to add his name to the

Source 3.7

The signatures on the Ragman's roll

roll. Indeed, as you will see in the next chapter, Wallace was more than likely an outlaw and would therefore not have been eligible to add his name at all.

'Toom Tabard' – Is this really John Balliol's legacy?

Historians have traditionally found it hard to rescue John's reputation or to put a positive spin on his reign. Certainly from King Robert's first parliament in 1309, the general trend has been to blame John for his failure to stand up to Edward, a trend picked up and enthusiastically endorsed by the fourteenth-century chroniclers and subsequent historians. Indeed, he was held in such poor esteem that no future Scottish King would ever bear the name John.

John clearly had many serious problems to overcome but even in his short reign he managed to summon annual parliaments. He appointed his own Justiciars of Scotland; one for Lothian, one for Galloway and one for Moray. He appointed three new Sheriffs for the west coast, extending the long arm of the Scottish King to the nearly independent Western Isles. He managed to silence the Bruce faction and keep his own close relations, the powerful Comyn family, happy. Had he had the time, who is to say that John would not have been able to disentangle himself from Edward's overlordship?

It is clear with hindsight that John was not a strong monarch, nor was he trained to be, but it is hard to say if another King would have managed to handle Edward any better.

The Reign of King John Balliol

Activities

1 You are working for King John on 1 July 1286. You have been asked to prepare a report recommending whether or not John should surrender or continue to fight.

- Recommend whether or not John should continue the struggle with Edward.

- Look at the pros and cons of continuing to fight.

- Can Edward be defeated?

- What might happen to John after the surrender?

- Provide arguments to support your conclusions.

- Identify and comment on any arguments that may be presented by those who oppose your recommendation.

In your report you must use extensive background knowledge.

You may be requested to present your report in a written form or as a spoken presentation lasting between 2 and 4 minutes.

OR

2 With your teacher's permission:

- Re-enact the humiliating ceremony that gave John his nickname 'Toom Tabard'.

- You should prepare a list of charges to be read out against John, and he should be allowed to answer them in an attempt to justify his actions.

- The re-enactment should provide factual information about the invasion of 1296 and the events leading up to it.

- It should also be dramatic and highlight the humiliation of the Scottish King.

4 **Wallace and Murray**

Early rebellions against Edward's rule

If it had been Edward's intention to settle the Scottish matter once and for all in 1296 he made a particularly poor job of it. With most of the Scottish nobility now held prisoner in England, Edward brought his own men to manage Scotland. De Warenne was named Lieutenant of Scotland and given charge of maintaining peace in the kingdom but he struggled with the job, mainly because he decided to return to his lands in the south, claiming the foul weather in the north would damage his health.

English judges (who had no idea of Scottish laws or customs) were brought in to replace the Scottish justiciars. Sheriffs were replaced with English lords. Many did not even speak the local language or care about the people or the lands they ruled. The Scottish nobility were likewise isolated from the community they had until recently represented and administered. As a result the new English administration in Scotland had a poor reputation and little or no connection with the native population. It was not long before reports were received at Westminster about the failure of Edward's officials to collect taxes or gather support from the locals.

By far the most hated of Edward's officials was Hugh Cressingham, the Treasurer of Scotland. Cressingham was the public face of this new and alien regime and his job was to establish an English-style taxation system with strong central government. Cressingham, however, soon met resistance and difficulties. He wrote to Edward:

> " *Sire, at the time when this letter was made, nor previously, from the time when I left you, not a penny could be raised in your realm of Scotland by any means until my lord the Earl of Warenne shall enter the land and compel the people of the country by force and sentences of law.*
>
> *Letter from Hugh Cressingham to Edward I, 1297*

Rebellion in the south and west

Under these circumstances it is perhaps not surprising that rebellions began to spring up around the country. What is surprising is that even Edward himself was taken by surprise.

In the Western Isles, the powerful McDougal family resented the rival MacDonald family being named as Edward's men in the region. In April 1297, the dispute became open warfare, and what looked like a local conflict threatened Edward's administration of the faraway provinces. More serious was the open revolt of Robert Wishart, Bishop of Glasgow, and the young Earl of Carrick, the future King Robert, in the south west of Scotland.

The nobles at Irvine

Young Robert Bruce (grandson of the competitor and known as the Earl of Carrick), and James Steward (ex-Guardian) had plenty to feel aggrieved about. They had not supported King John in his defiance of Edward and had probably expected to be rewarded. However, Edward was suspicious of both men. Both had controlled the south west and held important regional positions but Edward had relieved them of these roles and handed control over to the English lord, Henry Percy.

No doubt this encouraged Bruce and Steward to raise an armed revolt against Edward. Under the guidance of Robert Wishart, Bishop of Glasgow, the nobles gathered their men; however, the response from Percy caught the Scots completely by surprise. While the main English army gathered at Roxburgh Castle, Percy and Robert Clifford rushed north with a small army of knights and footmen. They confronted Steward, Bruce and Wishart at Irvine. Faced with such professional opposition, in early July the disorganised nobles decided to surrender without a fight.

Irvine has often been portrayed as a humiliating climb down for the Scottish nobles, especially for Robert Bruce, the future king. Some believe the surrender at Irvine was little more than political posturing and that Robert Bruce capitulated because he had discovered that Wallace's revolt was in the name of King John and had the intention of a Balliol restoration.

However, the events at Irvine did have two significant consequences. Firstly, the negotiations between the nobles and the English forces dragged on for several weeks. It has been suggested by some historians that this may have been beneficial to Wallace's rebellion because it tied down a significant English force that could have been hunting for him. If this is the case then it was not appreciated at the time. Wallace was so angry at the capitulation of the nobles and Bishop Wishart that he raided the Bishop's home and seized his treasury. Secondly, and perhaps more importantly, it left William Wallace in sole control of the resistance in the south.

Rebellion in the north

Who was Andrew Murray?

Andrew Murray was the son of Andrew Murray of Petty, King John's appointed Justiciar of Moray (and the whole of the northern half of Scotland). His father was one of King John's most trusted and loyal supporters. Sir Andrew senior held considerable political influence in the north and counted his brother-in-law, John Comyn of Badnoch, as his closest ally. Young Andrew was known to be trained as a knight, and fought for the Scots at the Battle of Dunbar. He was one of the many knights captured by the Earl of Surrey's forces after the battle and was transported south to Chester Castle to be held for ransom.

Source 4.1

An artist's drawing of Andrew Murray. Note the Murray coat of arms on his chest and shoulder

Source 4.2

Andrew Murray's northern uprising

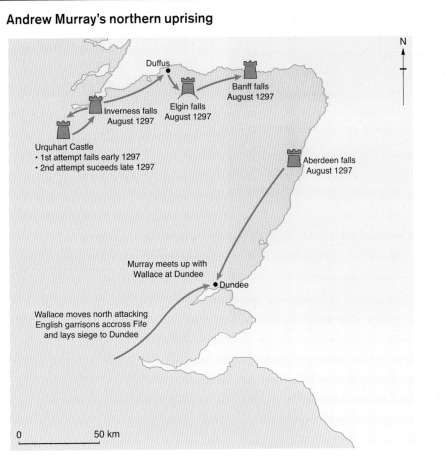

Duffus

Banff falls
August 1297

Inverness falls
August 1297

Elgin falls
August 1297

Urquhart Castle
• 1st attempt fails early 1297
• 2nd attempt suceeds late 1297

Aberdeen falls
August 1297

Murray meets up with
Wallace at Dundee

Dundee

Wallace moves north attacking
English garrisons accross Fife
and lays siege to Dundee

N

0   50 km

However, the ingenious young Scot soon found a way to escape, and made his way north through hostile territory to return to his father's lands at Avoch, north-west of Inverness on the coast of the Moray Firth. On his return, Murray found his lands held by an English garrison.

Murray's contribution has often been overlooked, but his rebellion in the north was probably more successful than Wallace's rebellion in the south.

Further rebellion in the south

Who was William Wallace?

Despite the fact that Wallace is better known than Andrew Murray, there is less historical information about the background of Scotland's famous patriotic leader. Documents concerning Wallace's life before the murder of the Sheriff of Lanark in 1297 are scarce and contradictory. What we do know would seem to point to a somewhat shadowy figure who was more than likely an outlaw living in the great Selkirk Forest.

Source 4.3

William Wallace

The 'Blind Harry' factor

Most of the story of the life of William Wallace comes from a poem written by Blind Harry in 1488, 170 years after Wallace lived. Little is known about Blind Harry, although people think he was a soldier before he wrote the poem. Although Harry wrote the poem 170 years after the death of Wallace, Harry claimed it was based on an older book written in Latin by a boyhood friend of Wallace, John Blair. However, his story is full of errors and inaccuracies. Such claims as Edward killing Wallace's father or that Wallace led an army to the outskirts of London or that he was seduced by Edward's French wife have no basis in fact.

The film *Braveheart* is based on Blind Harry's poem, rather than real life. Nevertheless, the legends and stories created by Blind Harry have coloured our views of Wallace even up to the present day.

There has been a recent debate about the name of William's father, and thus his social standing in Scotland. After his death, a genealogy of Wallace was created, clearly showing his father to be a knight, named Sir Malcolm Wallace of Elderslie. Neither this genealogy nor Blind Harry's poem effectively establishes Wallace's birth, and conflicting dates, including

4

Source 4.4

An early copy of 'The Wallace'

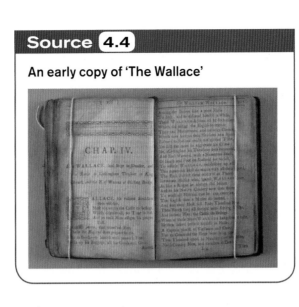

1260, 1267 and 1272, have all been offered as a possibility. If this is true then William would have been the youngest son of a minor Scottish nobleman. According to Blind Harry he was raised by his uncle, a priest from Dundee, who taught him French, Latin and Greek. It has also been suggested that William was not an only child as his two brothers, Malcolm and John, were both widely documented and both fought in the war against Edward.

Yet this accepted history of Wallace has been recently open for debate. First, the name of his father is far from certain. It is clear that Wallace's father was not named Malcolm, but Alan. Wallace and Murray's letter to the German towns of Lubeck and Hamburg after the Battle of Stirling Bridge confirms that William's father was Alan Wallace. Alan Wallace was listed on the Ragman's Roll as a crown tenant in Ayrshire, not Elderslie, so Alan Wallace would be of a considerably lower status than that of Sir Malcolm Wallace.

There is also a considerable amount of debate as to where William Wallace learned his military skills. Some historians have argued that he must have spent part of his life as a mercenary learning to fight as a common footsoldier. The only problem with this theory is where this training took place. In Scotland, a lack of any real conflict in the years before the 1290s would have severely limited the opportunities to learn military skills. It has also been suggested that he fought at Dunbar, but in truth the lack of any evidence makes this suggestion appear unlikely. Perhaps more probable was the theory that William Wallace was in fact an outlaw. Blind Harry offers a wealth of tales relating to Wallace the outlaw, portraying him as a sort of Robin Hood figure. In fact, stories of noble outlaws were very popular in the middle ages. It is not inconceivable that a young son of a landless family might have turned to crime to support himself. In Scotland around 1296 there may have been many such ex-soldiers or common folk in the same situation.

How did the rebellion begin? – The south

According to Blind Harry's 'The Wallace', the rebellion began with Wallace's murder of Heselrig, the Sheriff of Lanark, in May 1297. The reason for the murder is perhaps a little more contentious. Certainly Blind Harry, and subsequent modern myth, including the film *Braveheart*, points to the murder of Wallace's wife by the sheriff.

> After Wallace's escape [from his wife's home] Sir William Heselrig, by the failure to capture him, ordered the house to be burned and all within it, [Wallace's] wife and servants to be put to the sword. From that day Wallace vowed an undying vengeance against the English.
>
> Blind Harry, 'The Wallace', 1488

However, there is no documentary evidence that Wallace was actually married. Nor is there any real evidence for the murder of his alleged wife, Marion Braidfute. In fact, there is evidence to conclude that William Wallace was a known outlaw around 1296 and perhaps even earlier during the reign of King John. As a result, he would have been targeted by the local sheriff for capture and judgement. Perhaps this is a more likely explanation for Wallace's feud with Heselrig. It would therefore be reasonable to conclude that Wallace learned his fighting skills not by leading a patriotic band determined to rid Scotland of the invaders, but as a band of brigands and outlaws.

Regardless of the truth behind the murder of Heselrig, it seems to have sparked a general uprising with Wallace at its head. His band of followers was significantly supplemented by men from all over Clydesdale and the addition of the forces of Sir William Douglas. Wallace and Douglas quickly moved north to Scone to confront the justiciar of Galloway, Sir William Ormesby, a man almost as hated as Cressingham. Although Ormseby escaped, Wallace and Douglas arrived at Perth in time to intercept messengers from Bruce, the Steward and Bishop Wishart. Again it is unknown as to what extent these nobles had a hand in Wallace's rebellion, but English chroniclers make it clear that they believe that these powerful men were behind Wallace from the beginning.

> For the Bishop of Glasgow, whose name was Robert Wishart, ever foremost in treason conspired with the Steward of the realm, named James, for a new piece of insolence… Not daring to break their pledge of faith to the king [Edward], they caused a certain bloody man, William Wallace, who had formerly been a chief of brigands in Scotland to revolt against the king and assemble the people in his support.
>
> From the Lanercost Chronicle, 1297

The Scottish Wars of Independence 1286–1328

It is important to remember that the Wallace family's lands were to be found in the great estates of the Steward. Even when Bruce and his followers surrendered to Sir Robert Clifford and Percy at Irvine in July 1297, their possible co-operation with Wallace did not necessarily come to an end. Indeed, historian G. W. S. Barrow and some others credit Bruce's lengthy negotiations with Clifford at Irvine as tying down the English forces long enough for Wallace to gather enough support to make a difference.

The rebellion of the Steward, Wishart and Bruce still puzzles many historians. Why did they bother to rebel if only to surrender so quickly? Perhaps the memory of the defeat at Dunbar was too fresh in their minds, or perhaps they thought it was wiser to let Wallace and Douglas take all the risks. Whatever the reason, the actions allowed Wallace and his fledgling army to make it to the relative safety of the great Selkirk forest, which Wallace would have known well from his days as an outlaw.

Andrew Murray and the north

It is regrettable but perhaps understandable that Wallace and his rebellion in the south have gained all the attention in most narratives about the Scottish Wars. Blind Harry's poem has struck a cord with Scots throughout the centuries, immortalising Wallace's contributions, most recently in *Braveheart*, a film that all but erased Murray's contribution to the struggle.

However, it can be argued that Murray's actions in the north were as crucial to the Scottish cause as those of Wallace. Murray's escape and return to the north east appear to have coincided with Wishart's rebellion in the south west. It is unknown if this was intentional, or if the two groups of nobles were working together, but both rebellions appeared to complement each other. Murray returned to his family's estates to find them held by William FitzWarin. Gathering a force from his father's lands around Inverness, Murray unsuccessfully attacked FitzWarin at Urquhart Castle on Loch Ness. Cressingham ordered the magnates of the north east to capture and subdue the young Murray. It fell to the Earl of Buchan, still on probation, to capture his cousin. Buchan obligingly took an army west to Invernesshire and pursued Murray for a time, but without success. He claimed that his horsemen were no use in finding Murray because he took to the trees and the bogs to hide from justice. To English ears this sounded like a lame excuse, and Cressingham was under no illusion about Buchan's true loyalties.

Murray's second attack on Urquhart was more successful. Inverness, Elgin, Duffas, Banff and Aberdeen Castles soon followed, and by late 1297 Murray's forces had succeeded in driving out all English garrisons north of Dundee. By August he had joined Wallace at the siege of Dundee. Together

Wallace and Murray

they marched to Perth to plan their response to the Earl de Warrene's army that was approaching from the south. The Earl himself was absent, but the hated Hugh Cressingham was present. It was decided to meet them head-on at Stirling.

Activities

1 In this activity make up at least eight questions that you would use to test someone's understanding of why we know so little of William Wallace OR the importance of Andrew Murray.

This is not as easy to do as it sounds but it will enhance further your understanding of the topic.

- To construct questions you must first understand the issues you are assessing and ensure your questions are not vague or ambiguous and that they focus attention on the key issues. One word answer questions such as 'who was...' or 'when was...' are not allowed!

- Your questions should be mature, well presented and test real understanding. The purpose is to help learning, not to catch people out with really obscure or tricky questions.

- When you have eight questions, try them out on a partner. Can they answer your questions? And can you answer your partner's questions in exchange?

- The ones to remember are the questions that you could not answer. These provide a guide to the areas you need to work on a bit more.

Repeat this exercise either now or at a later date but this time your focus should be the other option.

OR

2 Imagine you wanted to make a movie about the Scottish Wars, particularly about William Wallace and Andrew Murray. When you come to sell your idea everyone tells you it is not a good idea because there is already a film about Wallace, *Braveheart*. How would you justify making a new film?

5 Stirling and Falkirk

Stirling Bridge

By 11 September 1297 the English army had advanced to Stirling and set up camp in the shadow of the great castle. Wallace and Murray's forces were waiting, hidden in the trees of the Abbey Craig, overlooking the Carse of Stirling and the only bridge across the River Forth.

The English army

Despite common belief, the army brought to Stirling Bridge by Cressingham and the Earl of Surrey was fairly modest for armies of the time. The English chronicler, Walter of Guisborough, claimed over 1000 cavalry (soldiers on horseback) and 50,000 footsoldiers were assembled for the battle, but this is almost certainly exaggerated. Hugh Cressingham wrote to the king to state that he had assembled a much more modest force of 300 cavalry and 10,000 footsoldiers, but even this seems to be an inflated figure. Perhaps a more realistic figure might be around 6000 footsoldiers when everything is taken into consideration.

On the whole, the English army that stood before Stirling Bridge was both smaller and less well organised than Edward's force at Dunbar. Similarly, many of the more able commanders and captains were elsewhere and de Warenne, the Earl of Surrey, was clearly not keen to be there. Hugh Cressingham was an able administrator but had very little military experience. There were two Scottish Earls present with the English forces. Cressingham had demanded that Scottish nobles turn out in the name of King Edward I to help put down this rebellion but only the Earl of Lennox and the Steward had actually arrived. It is unknown how many men they brought with them, but probably no more than a handful of personal retainers.

The Scottish army

The army Wallace and Murray had assembled for the battle was in essence very similar in appearance to the Scots army at Dunbar. The core of the force was made up from the followers that Murray had brought from the north east and Wallace's men from Selkirk forest. Additionally, they were probably able to summon many local men under the laws of the Common Army of Scotland. These farmers and tenants owed military obligation as part of their rent. It is impossible to believe that both Wallace and Murray could have managed to summon the local population to war without at least some support of the local Earls.

The majority of men would have been armed with pikes, mainly farm implements attached to long poles between 12 and 15 feet long. The 'pikemen' tended to fight in close formations. Later, the chronicler Walter of Guisborough called these formations schiltrons. At Stirling, the schiltrons were mobile and used their pikes effectively while charging. There were few archers in Scotland and they have traditionally been forgotten in most accounts of the battle. However, Wallace did raise a significant number of them from the Ettrick forest area, and it was said they were experienced with the longbow. Wallace himself was famous for his archery skills and his personal seal showed a longbow and arrows. Tradition and popular media often depict him using a claymore like the so-called Wallace Sword on display at the Wallace Memorial at Stirling. However, there is no real evidence that he used such a weapon and the Wallace Sword is in fact a sixteenth-century weapon.

The battlefield

Stirling Bridge lay in the shadow of the castle, over the River Forth. Wallace and his men held the high ground on the north side of the river by the Abbey Craig. From this vantage point he and Murray had a clear, unobstructed view of the English army camped on the Carse of Stirling.

Source 5.1

The starting positions of both armies

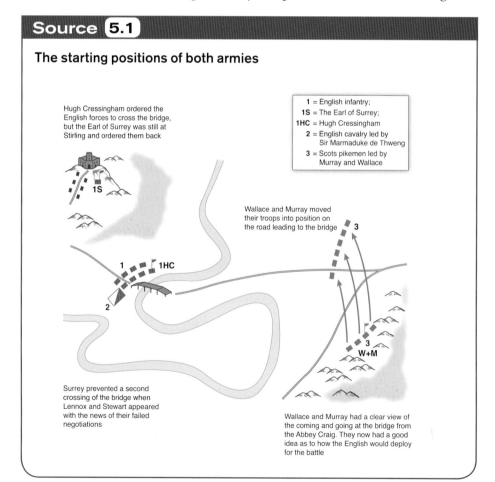

Hugh Cressingham ordered the English forces to cross the bridge, but the Earl of Surrey was still at Stirling and ordered them back

1 = English infantry;
1S = The Earl of Surrey;
1HC = Hugh Cressingham
2 = English cavalry led by Sir Marmaduke de Thweng
3 = Scots pikemen led by Murray and Wallace

Wallace and Murray moved their troops into position on the road leading to the bridge

Surrey prevented a second crossing of the bridge when Lennox and Stewart appeared with the news of their failed negotiations

Wallace and Murray had a clear view of the coming and going at the bridge from the Abbey Craig. They now had a good idea as to how the English would deploy for the battle

The main obstacle for the English was of course the bridge itself. Built of wooden timbers set atop stone foundations, it was capable of allowing only three mounted knights to cross in line at the same time. There was a ford a few miles away which offered an alternative crossing and Richard Lundie, one of the knights in the English force, suggested using this route as sixty men could cross it at once. Cressingham disliked this plan, believing that it would take too long to cross and would allow Wallace and Murray the opportunity to escape. Of course, Cressingham perhaps correctly assumed that it would have been suicidal to attempt to ford a river as significant as the Forth under threat of attack. The meandering flow of the river meant that there was always a possibility of the battle being fought in a bottleneck, and lack of space would decrease the effectiveness of the mounted cavalry.

How the battle unfolded

The night before the battle saw a small fight break out between the Earl of Lennox and the Steward and some foragers from the English army. This incident was enough to convince the only two Scottish nobles summoned by Edward I to leave the English camp. The Earl of Surrey had gone to bed early, tired and ill. When the English army began crossing the bridge slowly the next morning it took them a considerable amount of time to get men and horses over the bridge and form up in an order for battle. Unfortunately, because he had still not risen from bed, the aides of the Earl of Surrey called the army back across the bridge to await his presence. When Surrey appeared he ordered the troops to cross the bridge for a second time, only to halt the operation once again when Lennox and the Steward reappeared. Believing that they brought news of Wallace and Murray's surrender he called the army back to the Stirling bank. However, the Scots nobles only came to report their failure and their inability to raise any troops to support Surrey.

Source 5.2

An illustration of the battle unfolding

Source 5.3

The movements of both armies during the battle

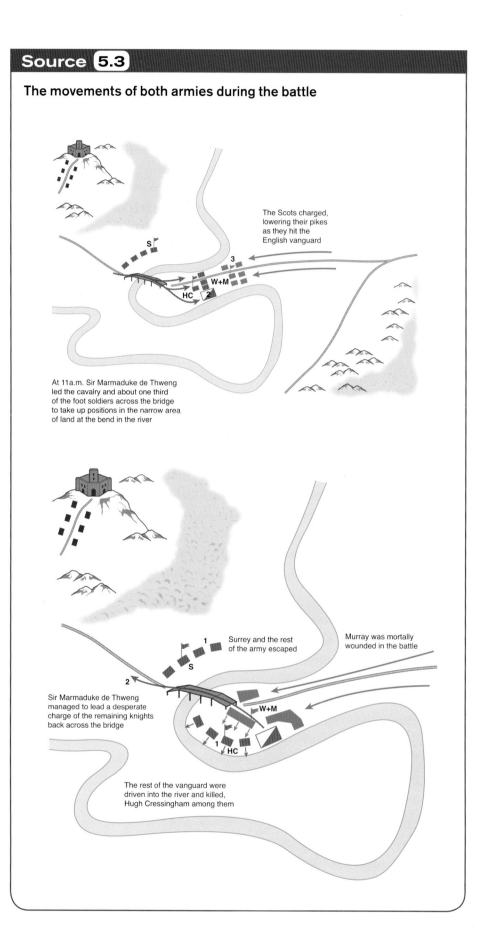

The Scots charged, lowering their pikes as they hit the English vanguard

At 11a.m. Sir Marmaduke de Thweng led the cavalry and about one third of the foot soldiers across the bridge to take up positions in the narrow area of land at the bend in the river

Surrey and the rest of the army escaped

Murray was mortally wounded in the battle

Sir Marmaduke de Thweng managed to lead a desperate charge of the remaining knights back across the bridge

The rest of the vanguard were driven into the river and killed, Hugh Cressingham among them

Meanwhile, Wallace and Murray were watching these proceedings from the concealment of the woods around the Abbey Craig. It was now very obvious to them how Surrey would advance using the bridge and how his men would form up once they crossed. Some English leaders now called for caution, claiming that if they crossed the bridge again in full view of the assembled Scots army they would be massacred before they could finish their deployment. The idea of using the nearby ford, so they could outflank the Scots with horsemen, was dismissed by Cressingham. Cressingham was anxious to end the uprising so he could dismiss the men in the English army and avoid paying any more wages than he needed. Warenne, the Earl of Surrey, agreed. He ordered the English army to cross the bridge for a third time.

It was around 11a.m. when about one-third of Warenne's army had managed to cross the bridge. The cavalry was led by Sir Marmaduke de Thweng and the constable of Stirling Castle led the footsoldiers.

Wasting no time, Wallace and Murray formed their troops into their schiltron formations with their best weapons and armour to the front. Then marching them in a steady pace they advanced towards the vanguard of the English army. As the Scots got nearer to the English the pikemen in the front ranks lowered their pikes, gave a great battle cry and charged into the waiting English soldiers. The English vanguard found itself outnumbered, outmanoeuvred and driven back towards the

Source 5.4

An artist's impression of William Wallace after victory at the Battle of Stirling Bridge

bend in the river Forth. Sir Marmaduke de Thweng managed to lead his cavalry to the safety of the other side of the bridge before the Scots seized control of their end. Now trapped, the remainder of the English vanguard was systematically butchered on the end of the Scots' pikes. Hugh Cressingham was pulled from his horse and, according to one English chronicler, flayed alive, his skin later used to make leather souvenirs for the Scots.

> ...the Scots caused him to be flayed, and in token of their hatred made thongs of his skin.
>
> From the Scalacronica Chronicle, mid-fourteenth century

Stirling and Falkirk

> ❝ ...[and] William Wallace caused a broad strip [of Cressingham's skin] to be taken from the head to the heel, to make therewith a baldrick for his sword.
>
> From The Lanercost Chronicle, 1297

Surrey and the other commanders, with the remaining two divisions of the English army, could only watch in horror from the opposite bank as the vanguard was destroyed. Very few of the footsoldiers escaped. Some tried to swim the river, but their heavy armour made it impossible and they drowned. Only about 300 lightly-armoured Welsh archers managed to escape that way.

Despite the fact that the Earl of Surrey still had a force that not only outnumbered the Scots, but in all likelihood outmatched them as well, the fighting spirit of Surrey had been broken. His commanders likewise failed to raise the morale of the English troops and they were even more dispirited to see the majority of the cavalry turn and ride as fast as they could for Berwick, escorting Surrey to safety. Marmaduke de Thweng was given command of Stirling Castle and ordered to hold at all costs. He was promised reinforcements but they never came. He held out for only a few weeks before surrendering to Wallace, providing him with many valuable prisoners for ransom.

Unfortunately, tragedy struck when Andrew Murray was wounded in the battle. He had been named Guardian of Scotland after the battle but his death in November was a huge blow to the leadership of the rebellion and to Wallace in particular.

Why were the Scots successful?

The great defeat of the Scots at Dunbar had convinced English commanders of their superiority and of the inability of the Scots to face them in battle. Even when more sensible English knights observed the battlefield and the Scots position they could not shake Surrey's confidence. After all, he had triumphed at Dunbar!

Hugh Cressingham's contributions were not welcomed by the other commanders. He had already reduced the numbers of English soldiers by sending many thousands of them home to avoid paying wages and he was eager to have a quick result to avoid paying more wages than necessary. Thus his insistence not to use the ford in case it allowed the Scots time to consider retreating, and thus prolonging the campaign, was an error of judgement.

The choice of battlefield was likewise very poor. The English had no chance to use their superior cavalry forces to outflank the Scots, nor did they have time to make use of their archers before the schiltrons charged. Similarly, the curve of the river and narrowness of the bridge meant that when the Scots did charge, the vanguard was trapped with no way to retreat or be reinforced.

All in all the English performed poorly at Stirling Bridge. They took no notice of the terrain and underestimated the tactics and courage of their opponents.

On the other hand, Wallace and Murray acted like professional generals. They surveyed the land and chose the best possible place to have their battle. Their timing was superb. If they had waited too long then they might not have defeated the English. If they had attacked too early then the vanguard would not have crossed the bridge and fallen into their trap.

However, the Battle of Stirling Bridge was far from a decisive encounter and in the long run had little or no effect upon the outcome of the Wars of Independence. In the short term it allowed Wallace and Murray, before he died, to claim leadership of the Army of Scotland and be elected Guardians of Scotland. It seems that the nobles were willing to allow them this level of authority as long as they kept winning and as long as they were doing it in the name of King John. Stirling Bridge proved that the Scots could, given the right circumstances, defeat an English army in the field.

For the English, however, Stirling Bridge became a stain on their honour that needed to be avenged. The Scottish victory had the effect of galvanising English feelings behind Edward and his new expedition to the north. Important English noblemen who were on the verge of open revolt against King Edward were now fully back in his camp, at least for the time being. In the medium term, Stirling Bridge may have actually had a detrimental effect on the Scottish position.

Wallace and Murray as Guardians of Scotland

Surviving documents that exist of the period between the battles of Stirling and Falkirk show a confident government headed by Wallace and Murray determined to carry on the notion of Scotland as a 'going concern' in the name of King John. However, it is likely that Murray's contributions were limited. He was no doubt in great pain from his wounds and died a few weeks later. In effect, Wallace was the sole Guardian of Scotland for this period.

Wallace had effectively taken over the leadership of the kingdom, despite his lowly birth. Why had the nobility of Scotland allowed this? There are several reasons. First, Wallace was obviously supporting King John so the Comyn faction was happy to allow him to rule. Wallace was useful to them. Any attempts to frustrate a Bruce revival bid for the throne was essential. Second, Wallace had control of the common army. The men had followed him and Murray into battle, whereas the nobles had either not turned out, or had

Stirling and Falkirk

surrendered at Irvine. Finally, if King John returned to Scotland then things would return to normal. Wallace had no future. If victory was to come the nobles could replace Wallace or work with him under King John or another monarch in the future. In summary, as long as Wallace looked like he had no intention of making a bid for the throne himself then the powerful families of Scotland were happy to allow him to take all the risks.

Wallace must have issued several charters and letters during his role as Guardian. Several survive and offer an intriguing insight into his governance of Scotland. One was a letter to German trading communities emphasising that Scotland was now open for business. It confidently proclaims the freedom of the Scots and Wallace's position as being subservient to King John. Another letter shows Wallace granting protection to monastic houses that recognised his authority in Scotland.

> 66 *Andrew of Moray and William Wallace, leaders of the army of the kingdom of Scotland, and the community of the realm, to their wise and discreet beloved friends the mayors and common people of Lubeck and of Hamburg. Greeting and ever sincere affection... We willingly enter into an undertaking with you, asking you to have it announced to your merchants that they can have safe access to all ports of the Scottish kingdom with their merchandise because the kingdom of Scotland, thanks be to God, has been recovered by war from the power of the English. Farewell.*
>
> Letter to the Hanseatic League from William Wallace and Andrew Murray, 1297

Soon all English garrisons in Scotland, other than Berwick and Roxburgh Castles, had fallen. Wallace led expeditions to Carlisle and Newcastle, burning, looting and killing as they trampled through the English countryside. By 1298, Wallace, now Sir William, having been knighted by the Earls of Scotland, was free to grant lands to his followers. Alexander Scrymgeour was awarded Dundee Castle and surrounding lands in exchange for his oath of featly to King John. How much power Sir William Wallace actually had remains somewhat of a mystery, but it is clear that he did enjoy the respect of the 'Community of the Realm of Scotland'. But would that support last if Wallace's luck ran out?

Falkirk

Traditionally, the battle of Falkirk is seen as a crushing defeat for Wallace. It has been suggested that Wallace was forced to fight this battle by the nobles who were not in favour of retreating in front of Edward's army. To

retreat would have been cowardly and not fitting for noblemen. They suggested that since Wallace was not a nobleman he would not be capable of acting as a gentleman, even in combat. Stung by these comments, Wallace decided to commit to battle and thus made the biggest mistake of his career.

At least that makes a good story!

The reality is that the events of July 1298 do not really fit this neat picture. As Edward moved his great army north into Scotland, he had no idea where Wallace was. His force had been unhindered in its march and he was convinced that Wallace had outmanoeuvred him and was heading towards Carlisle to attack the city. Edward's troops were running very low on provisions and his men had reached the point of open rebellion, claiming that they would go no further until they had a full belly. Edward had already made the decision to turn to Edinburgh to resupply when the Earls of Dunbar and Angus, both Scottish nobles who held significant lands in England, rode to Edward to inform him of the whereabouts of Wallace and the Scottish army. Wallace was north near Falkirk, preparing to shadow the English army as they retreated. He had no intention of fighting a pitched battle; instead he hoped to raid the English as they retreated, falling on their baggage terrain and rearguard. Edward made a hasty decision to turn north and surprise Wallace, who would think Edward was still heading for Edinburgh.

It would seem that Wallace had misjudged his enemy. Rather than being forced by the Scottish nobles to confront Edward, Wallace was forced to fight because the enemy were too close to pull back in good order.

The English army

Unlike the army hastily summoned for battle at Stirling, Edward had taken his time to gather his forces. Records show that 115 barons and baronets were in attendance, with large numbers of supporters. This would have given Edward a cavalry force in excess of 2000. Large levies of Welsh troops, many armed with longbows, were summoned from the south and levies from Lancashire and Cheshire, veterans from Edward's recent campaign into France, were sent north. Most significantly, perhaps, was the inclusion of Edward I himself. His determination to crush the Scots resistance, combined with his keen eye for battle and superb tactical abilities, made him a deadly foe.

The Scots army

Unlike Stirling Bridge or later at Bannockburn, the Scots army at Falkirk was well equipped with mounted knights; perhaps as many as 600 knights and squires. The Earl of Comyn, the Steward and other Scottish Earls had contributed large numbers of their followers for the campaign, although they themselves were absent from the army.

The rest of the army was deployed into three large schiltron circles, each with roughly 2000 pikemen. Closely packed, they presented a formidable obstacle for the charging English knights. In between these schiltrons were large numbers of Scottish archers from the Selkirk forest. Despite popular belief, these men carried longbows and were every bit as competent as the Welsh archers with Edward's army. However, they were significantly fewer in number, and could not hope to inflict as much damage as the English and Welsh troops. Some accounts suggest that Wallace prepared the land well in advance by digging in stakes in front of the schiltrons to provide extra defence against the charging English cavalry. If true, this plan backfired as the schiltrons were unable to manoeuvre to any great degree and were easier targets for the English and Welsh longbow men. However, many historians are unsure about the accuracy of this. Firstly, when would Wallace have had time to prepare the battlefield in such a way if he was surprised by the rapid turn around of Edward's forces? Secondly, it is unlikely that the stakes would have made much difference in dodging the hails of arrows fired from the English side.

Source 5.5

The starting positions of the two armies

Wallace formed his men behind a boggy morass which had formed between the Glen Burn and the Westquarter Burn. Recent rains had left the ground marshy and waterlogged. Wallace obviously thought that the terrain would discourage the English from a frontal assault. The Scottish cavalry seemed to be held in reserve on one of the flanks and there is little indication that they were part of the main battle plan.

The course of the battle

The English cavalry attacked the Scottish army on both flanks. Split up into two divisions on each flank they both swerved to avoid the boggy morass in the centre of the field and concentrated on the schiltrons at the end of the

Scots' skirmish line. The vanguard struck first, led by the Earl of Lincoln and the Earl of Hereford. They quickly intercepted the Scottish knights deployed to protect the flank. The Scots fought bravely but were quickly driven from the field by the superior English horsemen. So fast were the Scots cavalry defeated it later gave rise to rumours that they fled the field without striking a single blow. Once the Scots cavalry withdrew it left the Scottish archers without any real protection. The English knights were hidden from view by the large bodies of Scottish pikemen until the very last second and this left the archers exposed, leading to a massacre. On the right flank, the Bishop of Durham's force completed a similar manoeuvre, leaving the schiltrons without any protection.

Source 5.6

The starting positions of both armies

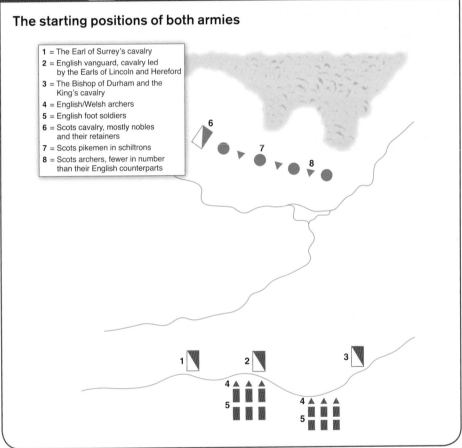

1 = The Earl of Surrey's cavalry
2 = English vanguard, cavalry led by the Earls of Lincoln and Hereford
3 = The Bishop of Durham and the King's cavalry
4 = English/Welsh archers
5 = English foot soldiers
6 = Scots cavalry, mostly nobles and their retainers
7 = Scots pikemen in schiltrons
8 = Scots archers, fewer in number than their English counterparts

Although it was impossible for the knights to attack the Scots, neither could the Scots inflict wounds on the English. Meanwhile the slower-moving English footsoldiers had arrived on the field and deployed opposite the schiltrons. The vast numbers of English archers opened fire on the Scots, killing hundreds upon hundreds with their deadly missile fire. The Scots could do nothing to answer this attack. They could only stand and absorb the losses. Unlike at Bannockburn, where mobility was the order of the day, it was this stationary positioning of the schiltrons that led to Wallace's defeat.

Eventually the schiltrons collapsed as there were not enough men still alive to maintain their coherence. The English cavalry saw their chance and launched their attack. English spearmen joined and charged into the mass affray, killing Scots by the hundreds as they turned and fled for the relative safety of the Callendar wood. Wallace and his commanders fled north to the Tor wood, burning Stirling Town as they went. Scottish chroniclers tell us that 10,000 Scots died on the day. While this is likely to be exaggerated it is perhaps closer to the truth than the claim by English chroniclers that more than 50,000 Scots were killed.

Source 5.7

The movements of both armies during the battle

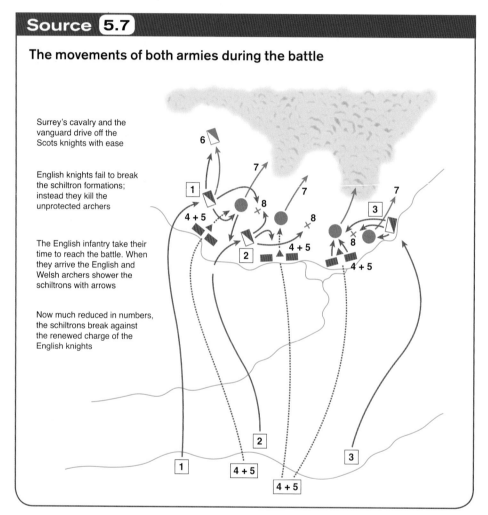

Surrey's cavalry and the vanguard drive off the Scots knights with ease

English knights fail to break the schiltron formations; instead they kill the unprotected archers

The English infantry take their time to reach the battle. When they arrive the English and Welsh archers shower the schiltrons with arrows

Now much reduced in numbers, the schiltrons break against the renewed charge of the English knights

Why were the Scots defeated?

The failure of the Scots at Falkirk has often been blamed on the traitorous actions of the Scottish cavalry running away at the start of the battle. This in turn led to the destruction of the Scottish archers and their failure to check the English archers from decimating the schiltrons. However, as we

have seen the Scots cavalry did not turn tail and run. They bravely engaged a larger body of well-equipped knights with superior training and experience. The outcome was never in doubt. The theory of their fleeing was no doubt created later as propaganda by Robert Bruce's faction to discredit John Comyn and his followers.

Again it has often been argued that Wallace was wrong to offer battle at Falkirk and with hindsight this appears to be correct. However, at the time it was not so clear cut. Edward's army was not so superior in number that it appeared invincible. The English were known to be weak with hunger and fighting amongst themselves and the effectiveness of the schiltrons against the English cavalry had already been proven at Stirling.

It was, however, the schiltrons' lack of mobility and the failure to protect their archers that was the downfall of the Scots at Falkirk. Despite what at first appeared to be favourable ground to fight upon, the morass did little to prevent the charge of the English knights. Instead it turned their attention to the flanks of the Scots rather than their more defendable front. The ground also made it impossible for the schiltrons to advance upon the archers as they poured their deadly fire into the mass of Scots. Finally, the schiltrons, unlike those at Stirling or Bannockburn, did not seem to be mobile in any way. Their defensive stance was their undoing. Wallace had spent a long time training his men over the winter of 1297–98. It is impossible to believe they did not practice marching in formation; therefore, it is a mystery as to why they remained so immobile during the battle.

Finally, some commentaries suggest that Wallace's poor choice of tactics at Falkirk reflects his lack of formal military training. They point to Murray's involvement at Stirling Bridge, suggesting that it was his plan that led to victory there. However, there is no evidence one way or another that Murray was a better tactician than Wallace. Murray suffered his share of setbacks in his short career and he himself had been part of the Scottish army's humiliating defeat at Dunbar, though he would not have been in a position to take charge of the army at that time.

The end of Wallace

Wallace resigned his Guardianship of Scotland not long after the Battle of Falkirk. It would appear that his authority lasted only as long as he was victorious. Without a noble heritage to fall back on or greater support from the nobility he had no long-term hope of political survival. He was quickly replaced by representatives from both the Balliol and Bruce factions. Representing the deposed king was John Comyn, head of the mighty Comyns of the north east, and close relation to King John. Robert the Bruce became joint guardian with John Comyn.

Wallace all but falls out of recorded history until his capture in August 1305. It has been suggested that he never gave up the fight for the restoration of King John. He supposedly travelled to the court of Philip IV of France and petitioned in vain for the release of the Scottish King. From there he may have travelled to Rome in order to petition the Pope for the same thing. Certainly at this time Pope Boniface VIII softened his attitudes towards the plight of the Scots and stated that Edward I had no business interfering in Scotland's internal matters.

Wallace returned to Scotland in 1303 and rejoined the resistance of the Guardians. It is possible that William Wallace was one of the Scottish leaders that routed an English advance near Edinburgh on 24 February 1303, although it is unlikely he joined John Comyn's army during the 1303–04 invasions. When John Comyn surrendered, after being offered lenient terms by Edward in 1303, all the leaders of the Scottish cause were offered amnesty with the exception of Wallace.

By the summer of 1304 the majority of resistance had collapsed and Wallace was running out of hiding places. He was eventually betrayed by Sir John Mentieth on 3 August and taken to London to face trial for treason. Edward was in no mood to listen to any defence. Wallace's claims that he never swore an oath of fealty to Edward and thus could not be tried for treason were ignored. After a mock trial he was sentenced to be hanged, drawn, quartered, disembowelled and beheaded. His head was sent to the Tower of London. The rest of his body was quartered and one quarter each was sent to Newcastle, Berwick, Stirling and Perth as a warning to those who might rebel against King Edward I.

Source 5.8

A memorial to the death of Wallace, near the site of his execution in London, now a hospital

What was the significance of Wallace?

Today William Wallace has a remarkable reputation: freedom fighter, warrior, hero, patriot and inspiring historical figure. Yet was this true at the time? Certainly the English chroniclers saw him as an outlaw, brigand and traitor. Perhaps more surprisingly, the Scottish chronicler Barbour ignores

Wallace completely in his epic poem, 'The Bruce'. It is only later that chroniclers such as Fordun and Blind Harry seem to raise him as a hero. It would appear that by 1305 Wallace had become something of an embarrassment to the rest of the Scottish leaders. His inability to negotiate a surrender to Edward and bide his time made him dangerous to the Scots nobles as much as to himself.

Some historians imply that Robert Bruce's rebellion in 1306 might well have been inspired by the brutal killing of William Wallace the year earlier. While it is somewhat romantic to believe this, where is the evidence? Throughout his career Robert Bruce offered only marginal support to Wallace's rebellion. Despite attempts to suggest that Wishart and the Steward supported Wallace at Bruce's urging, there is no clear evidence for this or any other open support. Bruce's surrender at Irvine coincidently allowed Wallace more time with his rebellion by tying down Clifford's force in lengthy negotiations, but perhaps it is a stretch to suggest this was done for Wallace's benefit. Added to this the fact that Bruce's murder of Comyn in 1306 was clearly an unplanned event, there is little to suggest that the 1306 uprising had anything at all to do with Wallace.

What then of the victory at Stirling Bridge? It is true that this was a morale-boosting encounter. It went in some small way to erase the spectre that the Dunbar defeat had become and showed that it was possible to defeat an English army with a set battle. Yet Falkirk was a disaster to equal that of Dunbar so how much of a boost to morale could Stirling Bridge be seen after Wallace's defeat?

It is assumed by some that Wallace's death caused widespread dissatisfaction among the general population of Scotland, but again there is no clear evidence for this. Records show no riots or uprisings in 1305 in Perth or Stirling where his body parts were displayed. Historians such as Andrew Fisher believe that the Scots were exhausted by war and this, coupled with Wallace's status as an outlaw, may well have led the population of Scotland to accept his punishment.

Yet Wallace's reputation survived long after his death. By the time of the chroniclers Fordun, Bower and Blind Harry, Wallace's reputation was one of hero and patriot. In order for this to have survived there must have been a strong support for him during his lifetime. Perhaps his sentence and death in 1305 did in fact mean something to the Scots? What was his legacy for future generations of Scots who read Blind Harry and had to contend with their own struggles with England? In the fifteenth century Scotland was locked in an equally difficult struggle with its southern neighbour. Perhaps the story of Wallace's unmovable and unwavering defiance had become more relevant and inspiring.

In the end all we can say is that for a time William Wallace was at the centre of defiance to Edward I. He led the Scottish resistance in the name of King John and was well supported by the common army of Scotland, if not so well by the nobility. At a time when the shadow of Dunbar affected the morale of the Scots, he and Andrew Murray brought back some pride into the kingdom with the victory at Stirling Bridge. And we know that future generations were inspired by his non-compromising struggle for independence.

Activities

1   Simple cartoon drawings are very useful to make sense of the happenings during a battle. Imagine you have been commissioned to do a series of simple cartoon drawings demonstrating the sequence of events at either Stirling Bridge or Falkirk. How would you illustrate the important information and how would you show the events as they unfold. Using at least four cartoons, illustrate the battle of your choice.

OR

2   Work in pairs or groups of three.

Design THREE word searches, each one no larger than 10 squares by 10 squares.

- One of your puzzles must contain only words or phrases linked to the main themes or issues in this chapter e.g. tactics or use of land.

- Your second puzzle must contain only words or phrases linked to the actions of the commanders of the English forces or Scottish forces.

- Your third puzzle must contain only names of significant people in this chapter.

- The words/phrases can go in any direction and phrases can be split.

- Each word/phrase must have a definition or clue to help someone find it.

- When you have completed your puzzle exchange it with another group or person and use the clues to the puzzle you received to find the answers.

Robert Bruce

The murder of Comyn

On 10 February 1306, Bruce and Comyn met to discuss their differences in the safe and neutral Church of the Grey Friars in Dumfries. It seems they disagreed, either because both wanted the Scottish crown for themselves or because Comyn refused to lend his support to Bruce's planned uprising against the English.

Source 6.1

Bruce's killing of Comyn is often depicted as an act of murder

When Bruce left the church Comyn lay dying. Bruce realised he had committed murder in a holy place, the greatest sacrilege imaginable. The story goes that Bruce staggered out of the church and exclaimed he had murdered Comyn. His friend and follower, Kirkpatrick, is supposed to have said, 'I'll mac sicaar' ('I'll make sure') and finished the job. Unfortunately, there is little evidence to suggest that this version of events is more likely than any other. The English chronicler Walter of Guisborough portrayed the murder as a cold-blooded assassination:

> Robert Bruce aspired to the kingdom of Scotland. Fearing the Lord John Comyn…he sent in deceit two of his brothers, asking that he would please come to him at Dumfries to deal with a certain business touching them both. Comyn, suspecting nothing came to him with a few men. When they were speaking together with words which seemed peaceful Bruce suddenly, with very different words began to accuse him of betrayal…but, as Bruce has conspired, struck him with his foot and sword and went away.
>
> *From the Chronicle of Walter of Guisborough, 1306–07*

The Scots chronicler John of Fordun tells a different story where Robert is clearly portrayed as a hero, while Comyn is the evil traitor of Scotland:

> A day was appointed for Robert Bruce and John Comyn to meet together at Dumfries. John was accused of treachery and he denied it. The evil speaker was stabbed and wounded in the church of the friars. And as the wounded man was laid behind the altar by the friars he was asked by those around if he would live, he straightaway answered 'I can'. His enemies on hearing this gave him another wound as he died.

From the Chronicle of John of Fordun, mid-fourteenth century

In the end it does not matter which version of the events you believe, the consequences for Bruce were the same. He had committed a heinous act, killing Comyn in a church. It meant instant excommunication and perhaps worse.

Now Bruce had no choice. After first confessing his sins to Bishop Wishart and receiving a full pardon, Bruce's followers hastily assembled at Scone on 25 March 1306, where Bruce was inaugurated King of Scots by the Countess of Buchan, a deed for which she later suffered.

Did Bruce have good reason to take the throne in 1306?

Robert Bruce's loyalties prior to 1306 have often been the subject of discussion. Sometimes he fought for Edward, sometimes against him. However, it is clear that Robert Bruce, the grandson of Robert the competitor, never swayed from the goal of his family – to gain the throne of Scotland.

Bruce had been named Guardian of Scotland after Wallace's defeat in 1298 but remained in the post for only a year. Comyn and Bruce had a falling out, probably over the restoration of King John. Bruce continued to struggle on in the south west against Edward's invasion but eventually sued for peace and guarantees over his family lands in 1302. As other leading Scots slowly accepted Edward's generous terms and promise of reform, Bruce became the leading noble in the pro-Edward faction. As the Comyns and Wallace continued their struggle after the winter of 1304–05 it soon became obvious that support for continuing the war was dwindling. Eventually John

Source 6.2

Statue of Robert Bruce at Bannockburn

Comyn was won over by Edward and the 'Ordinance for the Order of Scotland', which was published in Westminster in September 1305. This allowed Scots to once again become sheriffs, resurrected parts of the old Scottish government and restored lands to nobles who had fought against Edward. John Comyn and his followers were warmly welcomed back into the fold by Edward and heaped with rewards and offices in this new kingdom. As a result, Comyn finally abandoned his attempts to return King John from exile.

> " *An ordinance made by the king [Edward I] for the good order of Scotland. Note that our lord and king, in his parliament, which he held at Westminster…made it known to the good people of the land of Scotland that they should cause the community of the land to assemble, and acting together they should elect a certain number of persons to come on behalf of the community to the parliament at Westminster… It was there agreed that Sheriffs of Scotland should be natives of Scotland or of England and shall be appointed or dismissed by the king's Lieutenant.*
>
> *Extract from the Ordinance for the Order of Scotland, 1305*

Possibly because of his strong support for Edward since 1302, Bruce felt cheated. It was Comyn's followers who were named sheriffs, not Bruce's men. It was Comyn who was now Edward's favourite, not Bruce. By March 1305, Bruce had lost even his posts of Sherriff of Ayr and Lanark and there was talk about him losing the Earldom of Carrick. It is not hard to see why Bruce was feeling alienated in this new regime. However, was this enough to make him contemplate rebellion?

Perhaps more importantly were the actions of Bishops Lamberton and Wishart. Both were strong supporters of the independence of the Scottish church and in turn they were both supporters of Scottish independence. At Cambuskenneth, on 11 June 1304, the bishops met in secret. No specific details were written down, but it was clear that Bruce and the Bishops were to support each other in the future and if they broke the promise they would be liable to a penalty of £10,000. It was clear that Lamberton and Wishart now saw the restoration of King John as impossible and Bruce as the most likely inheritor of the throne. It is no wonder that Bruce thought he could act in the way he did if he had such important backers.

Early defeats

Despite the fact that Bruce had caught Edward's lieutenants in Scotland unprepared for his rebellion, his own men and his plans were equally far

Robert Bruce

from ready. Yet despite this Bruce launched several raids against Edward's forces in the south west and in Fife. He quickly captured the royal castle at Couper, and forced Comyn's supporters and family to pay homage to him. However, Edward had responded by appointing Aymer de Valance as his special lieutenant in Scotland. Valance had been Comyn's brother-in-law and thus held a special desire to see Bruce brought to justice.

By early June, Valance led a sizable force through Fife undoing King Robert's work of the previous months. In an attempt to crush Valance before he could raise enough men against him, King Robert rode north to Perth, hoping to catch him by surprise. Near Perth, King Robert's small army was ambushed by Valance as they pitched their tents for the night at Methven woods. Methven proved to be an utter disaster for King Robert and his army was all but destroyed. The king was forced to flee west with only a few hundred survivors.

Things did not improve when King Robert was harried at Dalry by John MacDougal of Argyll. MacDougal, a relation of John Comyn, blocked King Robert's escape route and routed his remaining men. At this point the Scots King ceased to have an effective fighting force. With only his closest friends and supporters he fled to the west coast and sailed away from Scotland. His wife, daughter and brother, Neil Bruce, were taken to the relative safety of Kildrummy Castle in the north east. However, Valance and the Prince of Wales had arrived with enough of a force to seal off the fortress effectively. Despite Kildrummy's formidable fortifications the castle soon fell, betrayed by a blacksmith who set fire to the grain store. The blacksmith asked for gold as his reward and he got it. King Edward despised all traitors and had liquid gold poured down the blacksmith's throat.

Edward's reign of terror

There followed a brief reign of terror as Edward's anger was unleashed. The Earl of Atholl, Neil Bruce and other leading supporters of King Robert were publicly executed in the same manner as Wallace. King Robert's wife was confined to a manor house and his youngest sister was sent to a nunnery in Lincolnshire. They got off lightly compared to the Countess of Buchan and other members of King Robert's family, who felt the force of King Edward's famous temper. The Countess, who had the misfortune of placing the crown on King Robert's head at Scone, and his oldest sister Mary were imprisoned in steel cages at the highest towers of Roxburgh and Berwick respectively. The Countess was kept like this until 1313, while Mary was not released until after the Battle of Bannockburn in 1314. King Robert's daughter Marjorie was destined for a similar fate – a cage in the Tower of London – but her sentence was reduced and she was also sent to a nunnery in Yorkshire.

King Hob

It is unknown where Bruce spent the winter of 1306–07. Some historians believe that he was forced to flee and hide on the remote island of Rathlin on the west coast of Scotland. Sir Walter Scott, writing in the nineteenth century, invented the story of King Robert and the spider's web to

Source 6.3

Bruce and the spider, an inspiring story, but not very historically accurate

highlight his plight and admire his courage and determination not to give up. There is, however, no evidence of the story existing prior to this.

Others put forward the argument that King Robert spent some time in Orkney under the protection of the powerful Earl, while other historians favour his staying on Skye, raising troops from the enemies of the MacDougal clan. English chroniclers do not give us a good idea to his whereabouts but they do award King Robert a new name. He was referred to, somewhat mockingly, as 'King Hob', meaning King Nobody.

Bruce's campaigns 1307–14

King Hob returns to Scotland

King Hob returned to Scotland in February 1307 in order to reclaim his kingdom. He first landed at his own earldom of Carrick and succeeded in capturing Turnberry Castle and raising a small army from his own tenants. However, success once again turned to defeat as two more of his brothers were captured and sent to England for execution. Undeterred by the loss of more family members, Bruce set up camp in Glen Trool in April, and defeated an English patrol that had been sent in to look for him. King Robert continued northwards with his small army and once again came face to face with Valance, this time at Loudoun Hill in Ayrshire on 10 May 1307. Despite Valance's forces having the advantage of numbers and a superior cavalry force, King Robert chose his ground well and Valance was forced to fight in a narrow stretch of land. Valance found himself forced to retreat to Bothwell. Several days later the Earl of Gloucester's force was similarly routed by King Robert, forcing him to retreat to Ayr.

The Death of Edward I

These early success may well have lifted King Robert's spirits and it encouraged men to turn out and support him. The feeling of hope in the Scottish camp can only have been further heartened by the news of the death of Edward I. Elderly and ill, he had tried to lead one final expedition to Scotland to deal with King Robert but he did not make it and died on 7 July 1307 at Burgh on Sands, only a few miles from the Scottish border. It was said that he made his son, the future Edward II, promise to continue the invasion. However, the Prince of Wales decided to take his father's body to Richmond and handed it over to the Archbishop of York before attempting to track down King Robert. Fortunately for the Scots King he had already decided to move north and the Prince of Wales was in no mood to pursue him. Instead, the English force turned for home and the coronation of the new King of England.

Scotland's civil war

King Robert had already decided to settle the dispute with the Comyn family once and for all. Only then could he win the support of the whole of the kingdom and make a united stand against England.

Bower tells us that the Bishop of Moray, David Murray, sent King Robert a letter promising that the people of Moray would rise up and support him with an army of 3000. It is unknown if this is true, but King Robert indeed travelled to Moray and spent the winter of 1307–08 harrying English garrisons and Comyn fortresses. We know a fair amount about King Robert's activities in the north east thanks to several letters sent to Edward II, first by the Earl of Ross in October 1307 and then by the Sherriff of Banff in April 1308. It would appear that King Robert's first major target was the Comyn castle of Inverlochy at Lochaber. From there it was a simple matter of travelling up the Great Glen, capturing Urquhart and Inverness with ease. This seemed enough to persuade the influential Earl of Ross to come to a truce with King Robert.

> *Be it known that we heard of the coming of Sir Robert Bruce towards the parts of Ross with a great force, so that we had no power against him, but nevertheless we caused our men to be called out and we were stationed for a fortnight with three thousand men at our own expense on the borders of our earldom... And Bruce would have destroyed them utterly if we had made no truce with him.*

Letter from the Earl of Ross to Edward II, November 1307

War against the Comyns

King Robert then turned his attention to Moray, first capturing and destroying Nairn Castle but then failing twice to capture Elgin. He then fell ill while attacking Banff. Sensing their chance, the remaining Comyn forces, under the command of John, the Earl of Buchan, tracked down King Robert's army to Slioch near Huntly. King Robert's men were dismayed at their leader's illness and some were saying he was dying. This dispirited group of worried and weary men were trapped in a lonely boggy wood. Edward Bruce, the king's brother, took command of the army and after a brief skirmish with the Earl of Buchan he ordered his men to fall back. It was here that Buchan made his mistake. Instead of pressing his advantage he fell back and regrouped, to return on 31 January. However, by that time the king's army had recovered enough to fight an effective withdraw to the relative safety of Huntly. Buchan once again withdrew.

Once he recovered King Robert pushed on with his attacks, taking Balvenie Castle and Duffas Castle, the fortress of Edward II's chief lieutenant in the north east, Sir Reginald Cheyne. Cheyne's efforts to confront the King appear to be only half-hearted and point to a lack of co-ordination between Robert's enemies, the English garrisons and Comyn's supporters.

The Battle of Inverurie

The conclusive encounter between King Robert and the Earl of Buchan occurred on the road between Inverurie and Oldmeldrum.

> The king came on with great strength, and they [Comyn] waited, making a great display, till they were nearly at impact. But when they saw the noble king come bravely on without hesitation, they withdrew a little on the pathway and the king who well knew that they were close to defeat pressed on them with his banner.
>
> *Barbour, 'The Bruce', 1488*

The date for the battle is rather unclear. Barbour claims that it was Christmas 1307, but this is clearly wrong and other historians, such as C. W. S. Barrow, prefer either 24 March or 23 May 1308.

All sources agree that the battle was a major victory for the king, who rose from his sick bed and was strapped to his horse for the fight, thus inspiring his men. Afterwards Robert ordered his forces to lay waste to the entire Earldom of Buchan as punishment. The Harrying of Buchan, or 'Herschip of Buchan', must have lasted for weeks. Everyone still loyal to the Comyn cause

was killed. Houses were burned and livestock slaughtered. Food stores were stolen or destroyed. The chronicler Barbour tells us that the effects of the 'Herschip' lasted almost 50 years. The result was the end of the Comyn hold over the north east. King Robert had almost succeeded in winning his civil war. The Earl of Ross eventually surrendered at Aludearn towards the end of October and officially joined the Bruce cause.

The south west campaigns

While the king had been harrying the north, he had sent Sir William Douglas to Galloway and the borders to attack the enemy castles and rally men to the cause. Their defeat of the pro-Comyn Dougal Macdowell and the capture of Douglas Castle led the way for the king's return from the north east and a new campaign in the Western Isles. The Macdougall family held power here and their loyalties were seemingly closely tied to Edward II. It is clear that the Macdougalls resented the authority of the kings of Scotland. Most of the Western Isles had only merged with the kingdom in 1266, and many of the powerful Western lords saw themselves as more independent than followers of the king of Scots. King Robert's campaign was fast and furious and ended with the battle of the Pass of Brander in the autumn of 1308.

The Declaration of the Clergy

Early in March 1309, King Robert felt strong enough to hold his first official parliament at St Andrews. Here he received the first real recognition of his title. The French King, Philip IV, sent an emissary to his parliament, officially recognising him as the new king over King John Balliol and asking him to take part in a crusade. Perhaps more significantly, Scotland's bishops proclaimed publicly Robert's right of succession, once again granted him remission of his sin for the murder of John Comyn and issued a declaration of joint approval of his kingship. The so-called 'Declaration of the Clergy' is perhaps an even more impressive declaration of support for King Robert than the more famous Declaration of Arbroath. The nobles supposedly issued a similar declaration, but it does not survive. The Parliament at St Andrews is significant in that it shows us how much of Scotland now supported King Robert by the end of 1309. However, it also shows us, by omission, that many powerful nobles were still against him, or at best neutral to his cause.

Source 6.4

Bruce's seat. Local legend has it that the king directed the battle from this stone, near Inverurie

1309–14

With the civil war effectively over by 1309, the war with England seemed to hot up once again. In 1309 and 1310, Edward II managed to raise enough of an army to march from Berwick deep into Scotland. However, King Robert refused to be committed to a battle, and the English host was forced to retreat to Berwick with the onset of winter.

While Edward wintered at Berwick, angry that King Robert would not commit his men to an open battle, the Scots were raiding across the border. This was a tactic that King Robert would employ often. Rather than risk losing everything in a single battle, he would force Edward II to retreat in order to protect the counties of northern England from attack. It was a brilliant plan that not only rewarded the Scots with the booty they could carry away from Northumbria and Cumbria, but demonstrated the inability of Edward to protect his subjects.

Between 1312 and 1313, the remaining castles still in English hands began to fall to King Robert and his commanders. Dundee fell in early 1312, followed by Perth in January 1313. Dumfries was next in February 1313, the Isle of Man in May and Linlithgow had fallen by September 1313. Edinburgh Castle and Roxburgh Castle were taken in early 1314, both by stealth. At Edinburgh, Thomas Randolph was guided up the north face of the Castle rock, by a local man who knew the climb well. Randolph's small force was able to scale the walls and seize the gate, opening it for the rest of the army to enter. At Roxburgh, James Douglas and his men hid themselves under black cloths pretending to be cattle grazing close to the walls before launching a night raid on Roxburgh.

Only Stirling and Berwick remained, and Edward Bruce's long siege of Stirling Castle had led to its commander, Sir Philip Moubray, agreeing to surrender the castle to the Scots if King Edward II had not come to relieve him by midsummer day 1314. Edward II could not accept losing Stirling Castle and the stage was set for the battle of Bannockburn.

Activities

1 The date is midsummer 1314 and you need more volunteers for the Scottish army. You have been asked to write a speech to encourage others to join up for King Robert. You are asked to inspire and enthuse the men who hear your talk. In a speech of no more than 250 words how will you achieve your target?

Or

2 Prepare and deliver a lecture to your class explaining why Robert Bruce had been so successful in establishing control over most of Scotland by 1314. Your lecture should provide context background, factual detail and a clear listing of the various reasons. Your lecture must last between 4 and 5 minutes.

Bannockburn

Source 7.1

An artist's impression of the battle of Bannockburn

The two armies

Ever since Barbour's 'Bruce' was written about 80 years after the battle, historians have attempted to determine the actual size and extent of the forces, their composition and deployment. Much has been made of the size difference between the Scottish and English armies. While this is true, the size of the armies had very little bearing on the outcome of the battle. In essence, more attention should be given to the quality and morale of the troops and the quality of their leaders.

The English army

Size and Composition

Professor Barrow's research into the size of the English forces at Bannockburn seems to indicate that the size of Edward II's host should number around 2000 mounted knights or men-at-arms and around 15,000 footsoldiers. Most historians tend to agree with this assessment of the English strength on the day. Pete Armstrong goes as far as to suggest that the number might be as much as 2300 knights but he also points out that this total represents the entire mounted force. The number of actual knights would have been much less impressive. Perhaps only as many as 800 would have been knights, the rest made up of men-at-arms and mercenary forces.

The bulk of the English forces at Bannockburn was made up of footsoldiers. Again the numbers of troops vary widely from report to report. The maximum numbers expected to arrive by orders of the king totalled more than 21,000. However, in the 1310 campaign, Edward II received only about half of the numbers demanded from his feudal levies. In 1310, many of the barons were unwilling to commit themselves entirely to the battle. Most sent only the minimum numbers required by their charters and stayed away themselves, instead paying the required scutage. (Scutage = Shield Tax, designed to allow knights or barons to avoid fulfilling their military obligations by paying an agreed sum that the king could use to hire mercenaries in their place.) As a result, it is safe to assume that only around 10,000 levies assembled at Wark-on-Tweed on 10 June 1314. Certainly, Edward II was worried about the poor turnout. He had already written letters to his marshals at the end of May to compel them to make sure enough footsoldiers would be available.

The chronicler Barbour makes a great deal of the foreign mercenaries at the battle. He mentions troops from French provinces such as Aquitaine and Potiou, along with German knights and Irish levies. There are no real indications of these mercenaries amounting to any real numbers and Barbour probably mentioned them because of their exotic nature rather than their military importance.

The Earl of Ulster did take part in the battle, and it is safe to assume that he brought a contingent of Irish spearmen to serve under him. However, of the 25 Irish chiefs summoned to serve, it is very difficult to determine how many, if any, actually took part in the battle.

The remainder of the English foot troops were made up of archers. Even by the beginning of the fourteenth century the importance of archers, and particularly longbow men, was generally accepted by all military commanders.

Source 7.2

A contemporary illustration of English archers

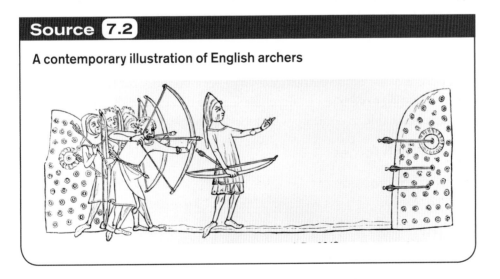

Roger Mortimer is reported to have raised 3000 Welshmen for the campaign and most historians have assumed that all Welshmen were proficient with the longbow. However, Armstrong points to the contemporary chronicler, Gerald of Wales, who claimed only the Welshmen from the south were accurate bowmen. Welsh troops from the north tended to fight with the spear. Of these 3000 raised for the 1314 campaign only approximately one-third came from the south. Thus we can assume that the numbers of Welsh longbow men at the battle were less than previously thought. Calls for archers from other regions seemed to have come to nothing, apart from 100 or so crossbowmen from Bristol.

Essentially, the English forces available to the English King varied in quality and for the most part resented their participation in the conflict. However, on paper the numbers still appear impressive and the recent history of encounters with Scottish armies would have given plenty of confidence to both troops and commanders.

Leadership

Technically, the English army tended to be split into three massive formations: the vanguard, the midguard and the rearguard. These divisions were often referred to as Battles. Each section was allotted an equal number of archers, footmen and mounted troops by the hereditary Constable of England, who was at that time the Earl of Hereford. It was the task of the Constable to make sure the forces were therefore ready for battle. The divisions were then broken down into groups of about 1000, each being given over to the command of a lieutenant of noble rank and position.

However, at Bannockburn the lines of command seem to have been blurred by Edward II's interference with standard tactics. He himself took no actual part in the commanding of his army, instead preferring to take part in the battle as a common knight. He appointed the Earl of Gloucester to the position of joint command of the vanguard, somewhat unnecessarily causing confusion and resentment. He similarly appointed other favourites to key positions of command, ignoring or removing more experienced nobles.

By the second day of the battle orders had been horribly confused, the chain of command was often unclear and the leaders bickered endlessly amongst themselves, unable to come up with an effective battle plan.

The Scottish forces

Size and composition

The size of the forces available to King Robert at Bannockburn is perhaps more apparent. Robert had plenty of time to assemble his forces and train them for the engagement. He had marshalled his troops into three large schiltron formations of about 1500 each. Unlike the English forces, these men were well aware of their role in the battle and had an effective chain of command. Barbour is fairly confident in his numbers for Bruce's forces – about 5000 men in total. While he may have exaggerated the numbers of English forces to make the victory more impressive, it is less likely he would have done so for the Scottish side. Medieval Scottish armies were not large. The population and economy of Scotland would not support large forces. Indeed, the 10,000 at Dunbar in 1296 represented a formidable host that was impressive because it was far from normal. Bruce's army was effectively a professional force funded on more or less a full-time basis so it is therefore unlikely that Scotland could have afforded an army larger than this.

Scottish knights tended to dismount and fight in the front ranks of the schiltrons. Note the long pikes in the background allowing more than one rank to fight at the same time

The majority of the Scottish troops fought on foot, wearing mismatched and scavenged armour and wielding the Scottish pike. The formidable pole-arm was about 9–10 feet long and had a sharp blade at the top. During the course of the Scottish Wars, pikemen were often drafted from the local population to create the 'common army of Scotland'.

Farming tools were commonly used when pike blades were in short supply. Any farm tool, from an axe head to a scythe, could be an effective weapon when the simple original handle was removed and replaced with a longer shaft. In Scotland, Lochaber axes, pikes and glaives were common in the schiltrons.

King Robert did have a few archers to call upon, and they were effectively used between the schiltron formations in order to provide more protection from cavalry flanking manoeuvres. Many of these men had no access to the mighty longbow and tended to use shorter hunting bows. While these may have lacked the range or penetrating power of the Welsh longbows, they were still effective at close range, and during the battle of Bannockburn close-range fighting was the order of the day.

There were a few hundred horsemen in the Scots army, possibly led by Sir Robert Keith. Their main role was to try to protect the highly vulnerable flanks of the schiltrons, whether from cavalry charges or archers. It is possible that James Douglas's men had a similar role and like Douglas, Keith may have fought on foot once the main fighting began.

Bannockburn

Quality and morale

Unlike the English forces who were marching north, the Scots had months to prepare for the encounter. They were also buoyed by the sense of victory. It had been a long time since they knew defeat under the leadership of Bruce. The psychological effects of Dunbar had, for a time at least, been erased. This was a well-trained and professional army full of confidence.

Leadership

Two divisions were given over to Bruce's trusted lieutenants, his brother Edward and Thomas Randolph, the Earl of Moray. Bruce himself commanded the third. Most of the other knights and nobles who took part in the battle fought on foot in the front ranks of the schiltrons, providing direction and focus for the common soldiers. The cry of the day was forward, and nobles and knights urged the commoners around them to press onwards during the fighting.

There is some debate among historians about a possible fourth schiltron formation led by James Douglas, the future 'Good Sir James'. Certainly, most traditional texts show him as being in command of this fourth division and restructure the numbers of the other divisions accordingly. However, the social position of the Douglas family at the time would not really have allowed James Douglas to command such a large body of men. Indeed, Douglas appeared to have led a small contingent of his own loyal supporters, probably under the command of Edward Bruce within his division.

Why then is there this confusion about Douglas? Barbour clearly gives him a more prominent role in the battle than he might otherwise deserve. The answer lies with Barbour's patron, King Robert II. When Barbour wrote his epic poem, Robert II was King of Scots and his family was linked to James Douglas. James Douglas was due to become an important figure and close friend of King Robert but not until after the Battle of Bannockburn.

Day 1: 23 June 1314

Historians are still unsure if King Robert intended to fight on 23 June. It is probable that he intended to survey the layout of Edward's forces before making any real decision. Regardless, Robert was determined to make good use of the land. Unlike Wallace, the Bruce did not dig in his men behind barriers and wooden stakes. Instead, he opted for a more subtle plan. Using the wooded hill of the King's Park to shelter his men and hide their numbers from English scouts, Bruce ordered the high dry ground around the old Roman road from the south to be dug up with a series of small uneven holes

Source 7.4

Battle day 1: the starting positions of both armies

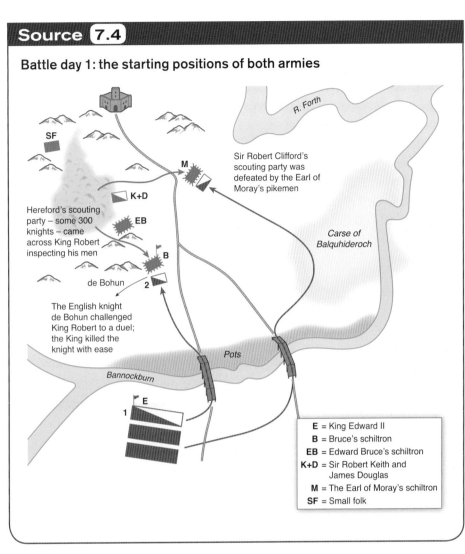

Sir Robert Clifford's scouting party was defeated by the Earl of Moray's pikemen

Carse of Balquhideroch

R. Forth

Hereford's scouting party – some 300 knights – came across King Robert inspecting his men

de Bohun

The English knight de Bohun challenged King Robert to a duel; the King killed the knight with ease

Bannockburn

Pots

E = King Edward II
B = Bruce's schiltron
EB = Edward Bruce's schiltron
K+D = Sir Robert Keith and James Douglas
M = The Earl of Moray's schiltron
SF = Small folk

or 'pots'. It has often been suggested that Robert intended for this to be a trap or deterrent against Edward's cavalry. However, this is just a little too obvious. By making the 'pots' obvious it encouraged Edward and his advisers to look for a different approach, one Robert would prefer.

The English force approached Stirling in some disarray with Edward unsure whether or not to engage the Scots on that day. Hereford, still smarting from his demotion within the vanguard, decided to scout ahead to determine the lay of the land, and make contact with the English garrison at the castle. Meanwhile, Edward ordered another force under the command of Sir Robert Clifford to scout the Carse to the east of the Roman Highway as a potential battleground.

Hereford's force of around 300 knights and men-at-arms moved quickly along the road, crossing the Bannockburn and moving towards the King's Park. It was here that they came across King Robert himself, inspecting his

troops and awaiting the return of his scouts. The Scots King found himself confronted by Hereford's force. Hereford's nephew, Henry de Bohun, saw a chance for glory and without waiting for any orders issued a challenge to the Scottish King by lowering his lance and charging across the open field. De Bohun thundered towards Bruce who sat calmly on his small horse. At the very last moment Bruce had his horse sidestep out of the way of de Bohun and, raising himself up high on his own stirrups, Bruce brought his battleaxe down onto de Bohun's head, almost splitting it in two. Henry de Bohun was dead before he hit the ground.

Source 7.5

Bruce duels with de Bohun

Hereford's force was then intercepted by Scottish pikemen belatedly arriving at their king's side from the tree line of the New Park. Despite their best efforts neither Hereford nor his knights were able to penetrate the thick hedge of pikes facing them. With his men falling around him, Hereford had no choice but to turn and flee, chased by the Scots cavalry led by Sir Robert Keith. The sound of cheering Scots filled English ears as they departed but King Robert found himself berated by his own officers. They were aghast that he had put himself into such a position of danger. Robert's only reply was that he had damaged his good battleaxe.

Meanwhile, Sir Robert Clifford's force had crossed the burn to avoid the 'pots' dug earlier by the Scots. Here they found the ground too soft underfoot but clear of the rather obvious traps set by King Robert.

At this time, the Earl of Moray, Thomas Randolph, had been ordered to position his men at the edge of the New Park, by St Ninian's Church, to guard the flank of the Scots army. However, the woods had covered the initial movement of the English troops and Moray was so late in responding to this that he assembled what men he had at hand and formed them on the open plain beyond the woods.

When the English force saw the Scots preparing for battle, an argument broke out among their ranks. Sir Thomas Grey, an ageing and experienced knight, wanted to charge the Scots quickly before they could form up in their battle line. However, Sir Henry Beaumont, another leading officer in Clifford's force, urged patience. He wanted more Scots to come from the woods, thereby making the victory more satisfying. Angered by this stupidity and ashamed at Sir Henry's accusations of cowardice, Sir Thomas

immediately set off against the Scottish pikemen. Clifford and the rest of his men then followed, charging Moray's pikemen without further thought of tactics. Unfortunately, Clifford's knights fared no better than those of Hereford's. They were unable to break the strong Scottish formation. Their lances were useless against the long pikes. In sheer frustration many of the knights tried throwing their lances, swords and maces at the Scots from a distance in order to try and kill them. They failed. Eventually the English morale broke and Clifford ordered a retreat. Many of the survivors fled back to their own lines, while others fled for the safety of Stirling Castle.

The news of the two encounters affected each camp differently. The English troops took the news of the defeats badly. Most of the footsoldiers had marched all day only to learn that Bruce had defeated Hereford and Clifford. Many knew of King Robert's reputation as a canny warrior and tactician. As the night went on and the story of the defeats was told and re-told, English morale began to suffer. Perhaps more importantly, the knights were angered and humiliated. They had been defeated by what they assumed to be a band of ill-bred Scots peasants. This would perhaps explain their over-eagerness to charge at the Scottish pikes on the next day of the battle. They should have learned the ineffectiveness of this strategy from the first day of the fighting.

The Scottish camp, on the other hand, was celebrating their victories, while at the same time planning on withdrawing northwards towards Lennox. Despite his success King Robert was still not willing to risk losing everything in a single engagement. It was the defection of a Scottish knight, Sir Alexander Seton, from Edward II's army in the middle of the night that changed King Robert's mind. Seton informed Bruce about the low morale and disorganised leadership of the English camp. King Robert must have realised that this was his moment: the Scottish army would fight in the morning.

Day 2, 24 June 1314

The night of the 23rd and the early hours of the 24th were very uncomfortable for the English troops. During the hours of darkness the entire English army positioned themselves to the east of the Roman Highway, with many crossing the burn to sleep on a slightly raised area of dry ground upon the carse.

As dawn broke, English sentries gave a cry of warning. From the tree line the disciplined formations of Scottish pikemen began to move down onto the carse and form up in their schiltron formations. Once the footmen had formed up into the three schiltron divisions, the majority of the Scottish knights dismounted and joined the front ranks of the pikemen. Then the entire army knelt as the Bishop of Arbroath and other clerics blessed the

Source 7.6

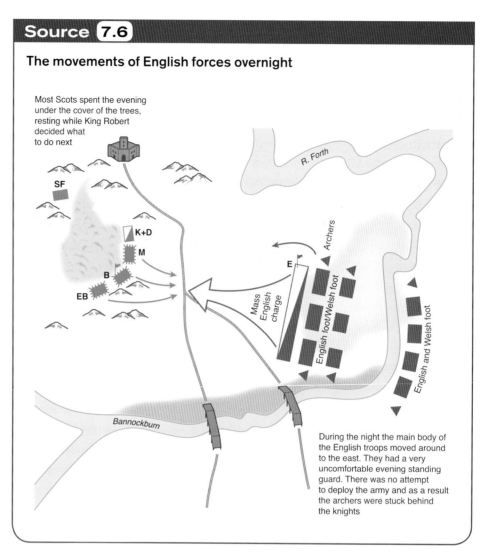

The movements of English forces overnight

Most Scots spent the evening under the cover of the trees, resting while King Robert decided what to do next

SF

K+D

M

B

EB

R. Forth

Archers

Mass English charge

E

English foot/Welsh foot

English and Welsh foot

Bannockburn

During the night the main body of the English troops moved around to the east. They had a very uncomfortable evening standing guard. There was no attempt to deploy the army and as a result the archers were stuck behind the knights

army using the holy relics of St Columba. It was said that Edward was amazed that the Scots would commit to fight, and he mistook their religious observation as begging for mercy.

The English army were not nearly so ready for the fighting. The Earl of Gloucester had managed to form the cavalry into a long line in front of the rest of the army. This ramshackle formation was pressed from behind by the footsoldiers and in front by the advancing Scots. The only realistic option now for Gloucester and his knights was to charge before they lost all chance of seizing the initiative.

In reality they had already done so as the two Scottish schiltrons were almost upon them. The Earl of Gloucester signalled the charge and was one of the first to hurl headlong at the advancing pikes. He was one of the first to die on the Scottish pole arms. The mass of English cavalry had learned nothing from the two encounters of the previous day. They were woefully

Source 7.7

The English cavalry makes little headway against the schiltron

unable to penetrate the massed ranks of the Scots. Scottish captains in the front ranks kept urging their men forward, slowly pushing the horsemen back towards the Bannockburn.

It would appear that most of the English footsoldiers were still on the opposite side of the burn, but some archers managed to make their way out to the eastern flank of the Scottish advance. They began to pour a steady rate of arrows into King Robert's schiltron, causing immense casualties. However, King Robert had held Sir Robert Keith and his horsemen in reserve waiting for just such an attack. Keith rode his 500 light horses into the formation of archers. The poorly armed and armoured bowmen stood no chance as the Scottish horsemen rode them down. The archers fled back into the ranks of their own men, causing even more confusion.

It soon became obvious that the English cause was lost, but Edward continued fighting bravely until the very last minute. Finally, a new Scottish force appeared on the crest of Coxet Hill. There is a great deal of controversy about the composition of this new Scottish army. Some historians refer to them as the 'Small Folk'; camp followers, cooks and huntsmen that accompanied King Robert's army. They had been watching the events from the hill, and when it looked like the Scots were being held by the English, they made make-shift banners, picked up anything that could be used as a weapon and charged into the battle.

Other historians have argued that this was an army of highlanders who had come down from the north to offer aid to King Robert. However, because they had arrived so late there was no time to train them in fighting with schiltrons. They would have got in the way of the well-trained Scots. King Robert must have kept them in reserve and had signalled them to charge at the most opportune moment.

Bannockburn

Source 7.8

The movements of both armies on day 2

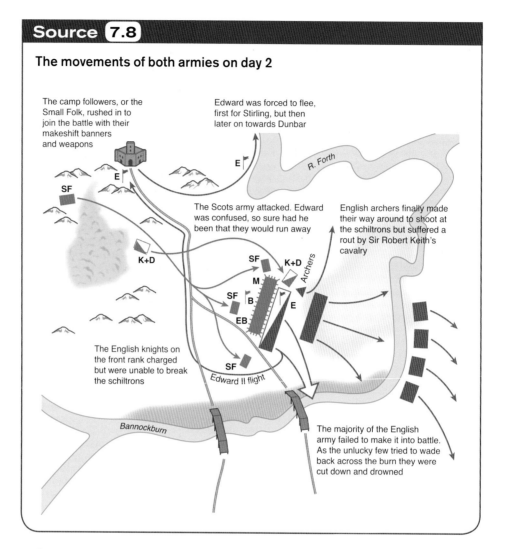

The camp followers, or the Small Folk, rushed in to join the battle with their makeshift banners and weapons

Edward was forced to flee, first for Stirling, but then later on towards Dunbar

R. Forth

The Scots army attacked. Edward was confused, so sure had he been that they would run away

English archers finally made their way around to shoot at the schiltrons but suffered a rout by Sir Robert Keith's cavalry

The English knights on the front rank charged but were unable to break the schiltrons

Edward II flight

Bannockburn

The majority of the English army failed to make it into battle. As the unlucky few tried to wade back across the burn they were cut down and drowned

Either way, the English saw a completely fresh Scottish army arriving on the field of battle. It was all that was needed to persuade those still fighting that the end had come. The retreat to the burn became a headlong route as men tried to flee the Scottish pikes. Thousands of English troops were killed as they attempted to cross the burn. Edward was pulled from the affray by his bodyguards and led from the field. At first he attempted to seek shelter in Stirling Castle, but the castle Commander, Sir Philip Moubray, refused him entry and Edward was forced to circle the battlefield before fleeing south towards Dunbar. Moubray was accused of being a traitor at the time, but he did Edward a great favour. If the king had sheltered in the castle he would have inevitably fallen prisoner to the Scots.

It is hard to estimate exactly how many died at Bannockburn. Several chronicles at the time offer varying degrees of severity for the English side. It is true to say that the battle was very costly for the knights and nobility of England, especially when you remember how unlikely it was for mounted knights to die in battle. England lost one earl, 27 barons and baronets and

perhaps as many as 375 other knights, although the number could have been as low as 154. Certainly, thousands of footsoldiers died on both sides, but several chronicles, including the Lanercost Chronicle and the 'Scalacronica' of Sir Thomas Grey, speak of thousands dying as they tried to cross the burn at the height of the battle.

> **"** In the leading division the earl of Gloucester, Sir John Comyn, Sir Pagan Typtoft, Sir Edmund Mauley and many other nobles were killed, besides foot soldiers who fell in great numbers. Another calamity which befell the English was that whereas they had only recently crossed a great ditch called the Bannockburn...they now wanted to re-cross it. In confusion many nobles and others fell into it with their horses in the crush, while others escaped with much difficulty, and many were never able to extricate themselves from the ditch. Thus Bannockburn was spoken about for many years by the English.
>
> From the Lanercost Chronicle, 1314

Reasons for the Scottish win

Edward II has often been personally blamed for the English defeat at Bannockburn. His limited grasp of tactics and interference in the chain of command meant that there was no real plan of battle. Added to this was the arrogant assumption that a push northward from Falkirk would simply sweep the Scots aside. Even on the eve of the 23rd Edward was unwilling to believe that the Scots would fight.

Added to this was the failure to learn from the actions of the 23rd. It should have been obvious that the Scottish pikemen were more than able to hold off the massed charges of the cavalry of England. At Falkirk it had been shown that a combination of longbow men and knights could destroy schiltrons. However, this lesson seems to have been completely ignored at Bannockburn and the archers were lost in the mass huddle of infantry troops that appeared to have taken little or no part in the fighting.

Finally, King Robert deserves credit for this victory. He seized the initiative and forced the English to fight on the unfavourable ground. His well-trained troops knew exactly what was expected of them. The Scottish commanders knew the plan and the cry of the day was 'push forward' and not to allow the English horse any room to manoeuvre. King Robert kept his cavalry in reserve to guard against an English counter attack, especially from the archers that could devastate his army. Some historians even credit the Bruce with using the 'Small Folk' at the right time to tip the balance in his favour.

The aftermath of the battle

The victory at Bannockburn was significant for several reasons.

First of all it represented Scotland's most significant military victory over English arms throughout the entire medieval period.

What Bannockburn did not signify was the end of the first Scottish War of Independence. It did not even constitute a significant defeat of England. England still possessed a more vibrant economy. The majority of the great nobles had not travelled north, or they had simply sent the minimum numbers required for the battle. Even Edward II had escaped the battlefield.

What then was the real significance of the battle?

In the long term it had remarkably little effect on the outcome of the Scottish Wars but in the short term its impact on domestic politics within Scotland was dramatic.

Scots who had remained unsure of King Robert now became supporters. Bruce's position as King of Scots became relatively secure. Victory had legitimised his claim to the throne.

Activities

1   In this activity make up at least 10 questions which you would use to test if someone understands why the Scots were able to win at the Battle of Bannockburn.

This is not as easy as it sounds but it will enhance further your understanding of the topic.

- To construct questions you must first understand the issues you are assessing and ensure your questions are not vague or ambiguous and that they focus attention on the key issues. One word answer questions such as 'who was...' or 'when was...' are not allowed!

- Your questions should be mature, well presented and test real understanding. The purpose is to help learning, not to catch people out with really obscure or tricky questions.

- When you have 10 questions, try them out on a partner. Can they answer your questions? And can you answer your partner's questions in exchange?

- The ones to remember are the questions that you could not answer. These provide a guide to the areas you need to work on a bit more.

8 The Final Stages of the War

Robert's Scotland

In the immediate aftermath of Bannockburn there was a rush by nobles who had previously supported Edward's rule to declare their allegiance to King Robert. This had nothing to do with patriotism, but plenty to do with practical reality. Edward had been soundly defeated north of the border and resistance to Robert was effectively over.

King Robert cemented his control over Scotland at his parliament held at Cambuskenneth Abbey in November 1314.

Here he passed new legislation forbidding Scottish lords to hold land in England. It was make your mind up time. Lords who held land in England and Scotland had to decide which lands they wanted to keep. If they chose their Scottish lands the lords could keep their titles and estates. If they chose to side with England they would lose their lands in Scotland. They would be disinherited.

Some of Bruce's most powerful enemies, such as John Comyn, had died at Bannockburn. Their lands were parcelled out among Robert's closest supporters, including Thomas Randolph and James Douglas.

For Robert, the victory at Bannockburn also brought him success in a more personal manner.

Source 8.1

Cambuskenneth Abbey today

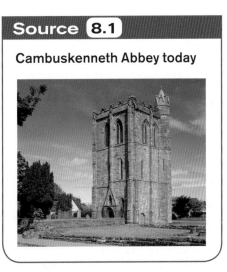

Source 8.2

The tomb of Bishop Wishart. Throughout his career he was one of the strongest supporters of Scottish independence

During the battle many prominent English lords were captured, chief among them being the Earl of Hereford. Such was Hereford's importance, Robert decided not to hold him for ransom but rather to exchange him for fifteen Scottish prisoners. Included among these were his Queen, his daughter and his sister, held in captivity since 1307. The deal also saw the return of Bishop Wishart from captivity. Now old and blind he remained a stout supporter of Robert until he died.

With the return of his family Robert could now set about restoring the royal succession, thereby securing his position on the throne. This meant it would be clear who would be next in line for the throne when Robert died. Meanwhile, Robert had not forgotten about the war and the fighting was renewed in August as Robert launched several invasions into northern England. Edward Bruce ravaged as far south as Yorkshire, burning and raiding as he went.

By 1315 Robert was unquestionably the King of Scots and few in Scotland would think about standing against him.

The War continues

The Irish Campaign

In 1315, Robert embarked on possibly his most ambitious plan yet. He sent his brother Edward to Ireland to establish a second front against Edward II. The plan may have started as an idea to put further pressure on the English King or to prevent him using Irish levies in future wars. For the ambitious Edward Bruce, however, it was a chance for a throne of his own.

Edward and the Scottish army landed in Ulster in the summer of 1315 and at first the campaign showed signs of success. Edward's early meetings with the Irish lords resulted in Edward Bruce being crowned high king of Ireland in May 1316. He defeated several English forces and managed to avoid larger armies sent against him. The Scots captured the town of Dundalk, a port used to send troops and supplies against Scotland. Edward also captured the main English garrison at Carrickfergus after a long siege.

Yet these early victories did little to establish Edward Bruce's long-term authority. Local divisions between the Irish chieftains saw Edward fighting many of the local lords who had only recently offered their

Source 8.3

Carrickfergus Castle

loyalty. Even the personal appearance of King Robert leading a fresh Scottish army failed to secure Ireland for his brother. Although the Scottish army marched across Ireland, devastating the local population, the Scots failed to capture Dublin or many other castles. After Robert returned to Scotland, Edward's only successes were the recapture of the Isle of Man in 1317 and retaining control over Ulster.

However, disaster struck in October 1318. Perhaps Edward's desire to gain some glory before a new army led by his brother King Robert arrived made him launch a rash attack into Meath. The Scots were ambushed by an English army at Dundalk in the battle of Fochart. The Scottish force was utterly destroyed and Edward Bruce was killed by a common soldier from Drogheda.

While the Irish campaign has been seen as a disaster for Edward Bruce, it was not a disaster for the Scottish cause.

The Irish campaign caused big problems for England and her struggle against the Scots. Military planners in England were worried at King Roberts's ability to take the war so directly to the English King's holdings in Ireland.

There was general fear that success in Ireland could lead to a combined 'Celtic fringe' alliance against the English with Irish, Welsh and Scots combining together. Edward Bruce even sent letters to leading Welsh chieftains promising his help in driving the English out of Wales. As a result, several thousand Welsh soldiers serving in the English forces were sent home for fear that they would rebel and join the Scots.

The overall effect of the Irish campaign was to make England divert a great deal of time and resources from the war against the Scots in Northern England.

War in Northern England

Despite the victory at Bannockburn, the war was far from won. Edward II refused to recognise King Robert or the independence of Scotland. The fighting was renewed in 1315 with an ambitious move by the Scots to take over Cumbria and Robert led a significant attempt to capture the important city of Carlisle. However, Scottish siege tactics were not well developed and despite establishing earthworks and siege engines around the defenders, the Scottish king was forced to abandon the siege.

Source 8.4

Scots siege artillery attacking Carlisle, from a contemporary manuscript

The failure at Carlisle did not dent Robert's ambitions and the years between 1316 and 1318 show a series of impressive attacks into northern England by both King Robert and his chief commanders. Famine in the northern provinces of England also hampered King Edward's desire to mount any serious threat to the Scots. Attempts to mount such expeditions were twice abandoned because of the lack of provisions. An attempt to take advantage of King Robert's absence in 1317, when he travelled to Ireland, was defeated by the hit-and-run guerrilla tactics of James Douglas.

In 1318, the war turned further in King Robert's favour with the capture of Berwick. After six failed attempts, the last major English outpost in Scotland was taken when Sir Robert Keith and James Douglas managed to slip in over the walls and capture the city by stealth.

King Robert followed up this victory by leading a large force into Northumbria, capturing the castles at Wark-on-Tweed, Harbottle and Mitford, while also capturing lands as far south as Newcastle. Scottish armies then plundered further south into Yorkshire, raiding the areas before safely retiring back to Scotland. Edward seemed unable to defend the north of his kingdom and local nobles and towns, forced to rely upon themselves, simply paid the Scots to stay away.

Source 8.5

The crumbling walls of Berwick Castle

The death of Edward Bruce in 1318 seemed to have lifted English morale and by 1319, Edward II was in York planning a major offensive against the Scots. By late August the English army mustered at Newcastle, and numbered 1500 knights and men-at-arms and in excess of 8000 English and Welsh footmen. Smaller than the 1314 army, it was still a significant force to send against King Robert. They marched north to Berwick, determined to recapture the important town and castle. It is probable that Edward II and his commanders hoped to lure the Scots into battle and gain revenge for Bannockburn. However, King Robert had already sent a sizable Scottish army south to Yorkshire. Led by the Earl of Moray, Thomas Randolph, and James Douglas, the Scots proceeded to do as much damage to Yorkshire as was possible. Edward II

had no choice but to abandon the siege at Berwick and head south to try and catch Moray and Douglas. He failed to do so. The Scots slipped back home not because of the approach of the English king but because, according to English chroniclers, they could not carry any more loot. Once again King Edward II was humiliated by King Robert.

Over the next few years the Scots continued to raid into northern England almost unopposed. In 1322, Edward summoned yet another great army at Newcastle, numbering almost 20,000 foot and 2000 horse. This was the largest army yet assembled by Edward but once again it failed. As Edward's army gathered at Newcastle, Robert once again seized the initiative and invaded lands around Carlisle before carrying on southward until he reached Lancashire and Yorkshire. Edward's army meanwhile bypassed Berwick and slowly lumbered north towards Edinburgh. But the King of Scots was not there to meet him in battle and Edward found himself lacking a real target for his campaign. Armies were expensive things to feed and pay wages and Edward knew he could not keep his army together indefinitely. Provisions had to be brought up the coast by ship, but a lack of ships and the threat of attack from Scottish pirates made it difficult. When Edward ordered his army to retreat and look for food, James Douglas led his men to attack the English column in a series of lightening hit-and-run strikes.

Upon his return to England, Edward II almost found himself a prisoner of the Scots. King Robert had heard of the retreating English as he was raiding in northern Yorkshire. When news reached him that Edward was at Rievaulx Abbey he ordered an immediate attack. Completely caught by surprise, the English made a stand on a hill near Old Byland. The Battle of Old Byland was another important, yet lesser known, victory for King Robert. The Earl of Moray and James Douglas led a charge up the hill defended by the English, while the Scottish king led his highlanders up a steep slope which the English thought un-climbable. The Scots drove the English army off the hill and they scattered. Edward II was once again forced to flee the Scots, barely escaping and forced to leave behind his baggage train along with his personal equipment and treasurey. Eventually the whole campaign was called off, once again resulting in failure and humiliation for Edward.

In 1323, the Earl of Carlisle was forced to enter into a local truce to prevent his lands from being completely destroyed by the Scots. This led to the Earl's execution as a traitor by Edward, but also showed the English nobility the reality of the situation. For all intents and purposes Robert was the lord of the north of England. The year ended with the English reluctantly agreeing to a 13-year truce with Robert, although crucially still refusing to acknowledge his status and the independence of Scotland.

The Declaration of Arbroath

While Edward II was unsuccessful in securing military victory against King Robert he did have much more success in isolating Scotland through diplomacy.

The English king was able to put pressure on Pope John XXII, whose personal lands in Gascony were still under the control of Edward II as his feudal overlord. Remember that throughout all his time as King, Bruce was still ex-communicated for the murder of Comyn and had been forced to ignore several orders from the Pope commanding him to reach a truce with England. As a result the Pope was already hostile to Bruce.

The matter came to a head in 1319 when the Pope summoned four Scottish bishops to Rome, presumably to explain why they had refused to carry out the ex-communication of King Robert. Bruce's reply was a masterstroke of international diplomacy. He sent three letters to the pope, one from himself, one from the clergy of Scotland and one from the nobles and freeholders of the country. No copies of the first two letters survive but the third from the nobles still exists, and today is simply referred to as the 'Declaration of Arbroath'.

The letter is an eloquent justification of Bruce's usurpation (theft) of the throne of Scotland and a firm commitment by the nobility of Scotland to support Bruce against the English '… for as long as a hundred remain alive'. The letter even goes as far as to suggest that if King Robert was to fail in his duties to defend the freedom of Scotland he would be replaced.

Historians have argued over the true meaning of the Declaration of Arbroath. Some believe the letter signifies the level of commitment and support King Robert enjoyed in 1320. It has also been seen as the birth of Scottish nationalism and the freedom of its people. While it is easy to see this interpretation in the stirring words of the document it is hard to believe that this was the intention in 1320. Most nobles would not have known the specific wording of the declaration. Indeed, it was likely to have been written by the king's legal clerks and the Abbot of Arbroath. Many nobles would simply have been requested to send their seals

Source 8.6

The Declaration of Arbroath

to be added to the letter. Rather than being an outpouring of support for King Robert, or a fanatical wave of Scottish nationalism, the Declaration of Arbroath was in fact a spectacular piece of royal propaganda aimed at gaining the Pope's recognition of King Robert as the true King of Scotland.

In fact, the actual political situation in 1320 was far from settled. Many of the nobles whose seals adorn the declaration were no doubt shaky in their support of King Robert. This is perhaps characterised by the assassination plot against King Robert, often referred to as the 'Soulis Conspiracy'. William Soulis's mother was a Comyn by birth and through her he had a very weak claim to the throne of Scotland. He had been one of the competitors in 1291. The true aims of the conspiracy are not clear, and all of those involved were Scots who had been strongly against King Robert before Bannockburn. King Robert moved quickly to put down the plot and Soulis was arrested along with the other conspirators. The affair did little to harm King Robert's control of Scotland, but does demonstrate that he did not have the full support of the nobility as was suggested in the Declaration of Arbroath.

Only a change of Pope and a new round of negotiations, this time conducted by Thomas Randolph in 1323, led to a softening of attitudes from Rome.

The Treaty of Edinburgh, 1328

The truce of 1323 was unpopular on both sides of the border and only lasted for three years. Many Scots were angered over agreeing to give up their conquests in Northumbria and the lack of recognition of King Robert by Edward. Meanwhile, events in England began to overshadow the war in the north. King Edward II, long unpopular among his barons and already having survived one baronial rebellion, was eventually deposed by a coalition of barons, led by his wife Isabella and her lover Lord Mortimer. Edward was at first imprisoned, and later horrifically murdered.

King Robert sensed the time was right to break the truce. He sent Douglas south with a great army intent on destroying as much of Northumbria as possible and putting pressure on the new English government. Mortimer hastily assembled an army and, accompanied by the newly crowned 14-year-old Edward III, raced north to deal with this threat. However, Douglas proved more than a match for Mortimer and the young king. Douglas's more mobile force refused to give battle, and instead taunted the English forces, riding rings around them and launching a night attack on the English camp that came perilously close to the young king's tent.

Meanwhile, King Robert launched another raid into Ulster, reopening fears of the 'Celtic fringe' alliance. When he returned to Scotland Bruce moved

south to lay siege to Norham Castle. Robert publicly announced his intention to annex Northumbria and began handing out lands to his nobles and knights. Although it was unlikely that Robert could have pulled this off, the seeming inability of Mortimer and Isabella's government to prevent it from happening was enough to turn the nobility against them. Hastily, in order to prevent another rebellion in England, Mortimer and Isabella let it be known to King Robert that they were willing to negotiate.

The resulting negotiations were ratified (agreed) in Edinburgh on 17 March 1328. In exchange for withdrawing from Northumbria and a payment of £20,000 in damages, King Robert was officially recognised as King of Scots. The independence of the kingdom of Scotland from England was committed to writing, signed and sealed. To secure the deal, a marriage between Robert's young son David and Princess Joan of England was agreed. Before King Robert died on 7 June 1328, he had lived long enough to see his final victory.

Activities

1   To be successful in this section you must be aware of King Robert's ability as a military leader.

    This activity will help you to select and organise relevant information.

    ● Write a heading: King Robert's military skills.

    ● Beneath your heading divide the page into three columns: Guerrilla Tactics, Terror Tactics, Battles.

    ● In each column list the facts you would include in a 10-mark 'How fully' question about Robert Bruce's ability as a military leader (more facts would be good).

    ● Shade each column a different colour (avoid heavy marker pens) to help differentiate them.

9 Aftermath

The significance of the Scottish Wars of Independence

The Treaty of Edinburgh in 1328 did not end the Scottish Wars of Independence. Edward III was always of the opinion that he was not really bound by that Treaty of Edinburgh as it was his mother who had signed it. Further attempts by England to assert its control over Scotland followed. As invasion was followed by counter attack, Edward III must have thought history was repeating itself. Again and again he had to intervene in Scottish affairs, just as his father and grandfather had done.

There were to be no more Bannockburns but Scotland retained its independence.

The relationship between Scotland and England was never easy, even up until the Union of Parliaments in 1707.

Even now English/Scottish differences are aired at football and rugby matches every year. Politically, Scotland once again has its own parliament and there are those who want full independence. The issue of Scottish identity and the relationship between England and Scotland is as 'live' as it ever was.

The Scottish Wars of Independence helped to shape the confidence and character of the kingdom throughout the later medieval period. Wallace and Bruce's names have lived on long after their deaths; their stories told and re-told over and over again. In more recent years films such as *Braveheart* have reinterpreted the stories, perhaps not very accurately, for a new generation.

To some, the Scottish Wars heralded the beginning of a strong Scottish sense of identity. The idea that the Scots were able to resist the influence of the English and retain their independence fuels the essence of Scottish nationalism. Edward I stylised himself as the 'Hammer (or destroyer) of the Scots', but for many historians those words have a different meaning. Edward I helped hammer the Scots into a nation. Others, of course, disagree. Some believe that the 'Golden Age of Scotland', under the Kingship of Alexander III, before the Wars of Independence, is more important in the formation of Scottish identity. Others believe that national identity is not something that can be said to exist before modern nations

came into being. Regardless, the debate over the importance of the Scottish Wars to Scotland's identity demonstrates only one aspect of its significance.

At the time, the Scottish Wars were catalysts in the growth of the importance of the 'Community of the Realm'. The need for the nobility, church and burgess to work together was essential in maintaining law and order within the kingdom. Similarly, the Scottish Wars showed a significant change in the nature of warfare. The importance of the mounted knight declined just as the impact of the archers increased. Gone were the ideas of mounted cavalry winning the day, as had been used effectively by England during the Hundred Years War. The usefulness of guerrilla warfare had been highlighted, as had the increasing cost of wars and the requirements of kings to have a more flexible standing army, rather than rely upon feudal hosts.

The Declaration of Arbroath has at times been said to have inspired the more famous Declaration of Independence of the USA in 1776. Indeed, its importance was acknowledged by the American Senate in 1998 when they passed Senate Resolution 155 marking 6 April a special holiday in order to celebrate the Arbroath signing.

It would seem that Wallace and Bruce will long be remembered as part of Scottish national pride. The first statue of Wallace was built in 1844 with many to follow. The statue of Robert Bruce dominates the battlefield of Bannockburn, and is seen by many thousands of visitors every year. The Scottish Wars hold a special place in the history of Scotland, and continue to define the character of the Scottish people.

Preparing for Paper 2 of the Higher History Exam

Paper 2 of your Higher History exam is based entirely on source analysis. The exam paper will be divided into five special topics. This book is about **ONE** of those special topics: The Scottish Wars of Independence 1286–1328.

What will paper 2 of my exam be about?

You have to answer ONE special topic section.

You must answer the questions set on the special topic you have studied.

There will be questions on other special topics that other candidates have studied. Make sure you answer the correct special topic.

Your special topic syllabus is divided into six main sections.

Check out the syllabus at http://www.sqa.org.uk. Scroll down to page 44 to see the detailed content of special topic 'The Scottish Wars of Independence 1286–1328'.

The first section you will see is called 'Background'. The last section is called 'Perspective'. Neither of those sections will have any questions asked about them. They are **NOT** examined. That leaves four other sections, called issues, and each one of those issues has a question linked to it.

What do I have to do?

You will have five sources to use and four questions to answer. You will have 1 hour and 25 minutes to do that. That means you will have about 20 minutes to deal with each question so answers must be well structured and well developed. Put simply, that means you must do three things in each question:

1. **You must do what you are asked to do.**
2. **You must refer to information in the source.**
3. **You must also include your own relevant recalled knowledge.**

Each question also has its own particular process you must use to answer it successfully.

Later in this chapter there are sample answers to show you how to deal with the different questions.

What types of questions will I be asked?

There are **FOUR** different types of question. Each type will be in your exam paper.

Important: In this book the questions are listed as Type 1, 2, 3 and 4. This does not mean the questions will appear in that order in the exam. The different types of questions can appear in any order.

> Question Type 1 is a Source Evaluation Question worth 5 Marks.

It will usually be identified with a question asking 'How useful is Source A as evidence ...?'

In this type of question you are being asked to **judge** how good the source is as a piece of **historical evidence**:

- You will get up to a maximum of **2 marks** for writing about the source's origin (who wrote it or where the source first appeared) and its purpose (why the source was produced).

- You will only get up to **1 mark** by identifying and commenting briefly on where the source is from and why it was produced.

- For **2 marks** you will be expected to explain why its origin and purpose is important in the context of the question.

You will get up to a maximum of **2 marks** for **explaining why** the parts of the source you have selected are **useful** in terms of the question:

- There are no marks for just copying chunks of the source.

- Just listing relevant points from the source will only gain **1 mark**.

- For **2 marks** you must mention a point from the source and ALSO explain why the evidence you have selected is relevant to the question.

- Watch out for how that works in the examples that follow.

You will get up to a maximum of **2 marks** for using your own **detailed knowledge** as long as it is relevant to the question. This is called using relevant recall:

- You might, for example, want to consider if the source is entirely useful. A source will seldom be entirely valuable or useful. It will have limitations and it's up to you to explain what these limits to usefulness are.

- In this case a useful word to use is '**partly**'!

- You can give evidence to show that the source has its uses but also include information to suggest the source does not give the whole picture.

This looks like the total number of marks available for the question comes to 6, but there is only a possible total of 5 marks for this question. Stop to think how this helps you. If you had a weak section on origin and purpose you might only get 1 mark out of 2. But if your other two sections are well done, gaining the maximum of 2 marks per part, then you can still achieve the maximum total of 5 marks.

> **Question Type 2 is a comparison question worth 5 marks.**

You will be asked to compare two points of view overall and in detail. It might **NOT** use the word 'compare' in the question.

The wording of the question might be something like 'To what extent does Source B agree with Source C about...?'

You will get up to a maximum of **2 marks** for an **overall comparison**. That means you should outline the main ideas or opinions or points of view in the two sources.

You will get up to a maximum of **4 marks** by **developing** your comparison in **detail**.

To get all 4 marks it is *not enough* just to list points of difference between the sources. In fact you might get **NO MARKS** for simply stating 'Source B says... but Source C says...'

- You **MUST** show that you understand the points made in the sources and explain in what ways they differ from each other or support each other.

- When you are explaining the differences or similarities it would be a good idea to use your own detailed knowledge to support your answer.

- There will always be **4** points of comparison for you to find in the sources.

- You will get **NO MARKS** for 'ghost' comparisons. In other words, no marks for writing 'Source B says... but Source C makes no mention of this.'

> **Question Type 3 is a 'How far' question and is worth 10 marks.**

This question is to test your knowledge on one specific part of an issue, called a sub-issue. You can find all the sub-issues in the column called 'detailed descriptors' on the SQA syllabus website. The web address is given earlier in this chapter.

For example, a question that asks, 'How far does Source B explain the reasons why the Scots asked for help from Edward I in 1286?' tests your knowledge of the reasons for Scots' concerns of unrest after the death of Alexander III.

To answer this question you must show you have **understood the reasons** why the Scots asked King Edward to help them find a new king – these are included in the source – and be able to explain those reasons. You can get up to **4 marks** just by doing that.

You must **ALSO** include as much **accurate and relevant information** from your **own knowledge** about why the Scots felt they needed to turn to an outside power to help them settle the succession crises. You can get up to **7 marks** for this part of your answer.

As you write, ask yourself if the information you are including helps to answer the question to reach a balanced answer – or are you just including stuff you know without really thinking about whether it answers the question?

(?) **What is recall?**

Recall means the detailed, factual information you know about a certain topic. When evaluating a source, recall can mean using your knowledge to explain more fully a point already made in the source. It does not always have to be a completely new point.

> Question Type 4 is a 'How fully' question and is worth 10 marks.

This question is to test your knowledge of a whole issue. Remember there are four issues in the syllabus that can be examined.

It could ask 'How fully does Source A illustrate the impact of the succession crises in Scotland in 1286–96?' The words 'succession crises in Scotland in 1286–96' come straight from the issue title in the syllabus.

Just as in the other 10 mark question, you can get up to **4 marks** for **explaining** the points in the source **relevant to the question.** You can then get up to **7 marks** for relevant **detailed recall** that helps answer the question directly.

Now do some training!

Read this before you start answering questions. It will help you to improve your answers.

Activities 📝

1 After each worked example you will see another question for you to try yourself. Read again the advice about writing a good answer.

2 Write your answer.

3 Exchange your answer with a partner. Use the information you already have about how marks are given to judge the value of your partner's answer. Return the marked answer. If there is any disagreement or difficulty ask your teacher to referee!

4 Once you have agreed the final mark take time to think about why you got the mark you did. Make two columns. Title one column 'What I did well'. Title the other column 'What I could improve on'. Use the feedback from your partner, your teacher and your own thoughts about your mark to complete the columns. Next time you do this type of question remember these columns!

The reason for doing this exercise is to understand and use the mark scheme. Once you know how marks are given you can structure your own answers to provide what markers are looking for.

Question Type 1 – Source Evaluation

Source A is from a letter written by Robert Bruce on behalf of the seven Earls of Scotland explaining why they wish Edward I to intervene in the succession, written sometime between 1290 and 1291.

Source A

Since the death of Lord Alexander, late king of Scotland, the royal throne of the kingdom has been vacant until the present time and by the laws and customs of the kingdom of Scotland it is one of the rights and privileges of the seven earls of the kingdom of Scotland and of the community of the realm to make a king and set him upon the royal throne.

In the name of the said earls, the bishops, abbots, priors, barons and free tenants of Scotland appeal by this document to the Lord Edward, king of England. I seek urgently the help of the king of England in placing the seven earls and the community of the realm under the special peace and protection of the king of England.

Though we, Robert Bruce, as the legitimate and true heir to rule the realm of Scotland, have put forward a claim concerning the right to Scotland, William Fraser, bishop of St Andrew and John Comyn, along with others who support them and agree with what they want intend to propose to make John Balliol king.

> How useful is Source A as evidence of the problems caused by the death of the Maid of Norway? **(5 marks)**

Here is a weak answer:

The source is useful because it gives a description of the problems facing Scotland after the death of the Maid of Norway. It says that there has been no king 'since the death of Lord Alexander'. It shows how Robert Bruce has asked for Edward to protect the peace of Scotland. It shows that Bishop Fraser and John Comyn do not support Robert Bruce and his plans. The source is useful because it shows that the nobles of Scotland are getting ready for a civil war, as both John Balliol and Robert Bruce want to be king of Scots.

Why is this a weak answer?

This answer is weak mainly because:

(1) The answer fails to evaluate by referring to the origins and possible purpose of the source.

(2) The answer just describes the source.

(3) The answer is useful in the detail it gives of political arguments in Scotland but mainly it just copies large sections of the source.

(4) The answer contains no recalled knowledge.

(5) There is no attempt to provide a balanced answer suggesting the source might have its limits as a useful piece of evidence.

Marks

- There is no attempt to deal with origin or purpose (0 marks).

- It selects some relevant information from the source. However, it just lists some relevant points from the source. It does not explain why the evidence selected is relevant to the question (1 mark).

- There is no recall (0 marks).

Total achieved: 1 mark out of 5.

Here is a much better answer:

This source is partly useful for finding out about the problems faced by Scotland after the death of the Maid of Norway but it has limits.

The source is written by Robert Bruce sometime between 1290 and 1291 so is written by an eyewitness who not only sees first hand what the problems in Scotland are, but has some involvement in the creation of the problems. The purpose of the source is to try and persuade Edward I that Robert and not John Balliol should be king and that Andrew Fraser and John Comyn are the troublemakers. This makes the source very useful as primary evidence giving a first-hand account of the arguments between the nobles. As it is a letter hoping to win over Edward I to his side it is likely only to tell Edward good things about Robert I and place the blame for troubles on Robert's enemies.

The detail given matches with my own knowledge. The source is correct in saying that Andrew Fisher wanted Balliol to be king. He wrote to Edward in 1290 asking to come to an arrangement with Balliol. The source is also correct in saying that Robert Bruce and John Balliol both wanted to be king.

However, the source does have its limits. It doesn't say that it was not John Balliol who started the trouble. Robert Bruce had already captured castles like Dumfries and Wigtown after Alexander's death. There is also no evidence from the source to show that in fact there was very little unrest outside the Bruce's lands and that the community of the realm kept the peace of Scotland fairly well.

Overall the source is quite useful for giving an impression of the problems of Scotland but it is very one sided and you would have to read sources written by the Balliol faction to get a better idea of Scotland's problems and who was to blame.

Why is this a much better answer?

It is a better answer because:

(1) It not only identifies the origin and purpose of the source but explains why each makes it a useful source (2 marks).

(2) It provides detail of Scotland's problems which matches other reports and gives a first-hand report of the arguments between the nobles. It also shows how Robert Bruce feels about Balliol's claim and this answer does make clear how the evidence selected is relevant to the question (2 marks).

(3) The source provides a balanced evaluation of the usefulness of the source and includes more recall that helps evaluate the evidence in terms of the question asked (2 marks).

Marks

This answer scores highly simply by following the three stage marking scheme process. The maximum number of marks for a Type 1 question is 5 so even if this answer dropped a mark on a section, the writer would still gain full marks.

Now try it yourself

Source B is from a letter by King John to King Edward, asking him to grant him leave of absence from the English Parliament at York on 29 April 1293.

> ### Source B
>
> When from a report of some of our people we learned that your justiciars shall be judging cases in the county of York fifteen days after Trinity next, and since in your last parliament at Newcastle upon Tyne we made requests of your lordship about having exception from attending that common summons at York, you then promised permission. We now cordially seek again the kindness we have already experienced and ask that, if it pleases you, to remember that promise and, if you judge it right to do so, grant that exemption officially. We find you as always kind and generous.

How useful is Source B in explaining the problems faced by King John after he became King of Scots in 1292? **(5 marks)**

You should refer to:

- *the origin and possible purpose of the source*
- *the content of the source*
- *recalled knowledge.*

Question Type 2 – The Comparison Question

Source A is a description of Edward I's assault on the Castle of Caerlaverock in 1300, taken from *A Great and Terrible King: Edward I and the Forging of Britain*, by Marc Morris (2008).

Source A

His first target was Caerlaverock Castle, which lay just a few miles across the Border on the opposite shore of the Solway Firth. This castle and its small Scottish garrison had been making life miserable for their English neighbours at Dumfries and Lochmaben. Their ability to resist a large army, however, was limited: Caerlaverock is no Stirling. The newly built home of a prosperous local knight, it had been designed with the intention of keeping out local raiders, not repelling a wrathful English king. For a few days in July 1300 its defenders manfully withstood some showy assaults by the English knights, but once Edward's fleet arrived with his heavy siege equipment, they recognised that the game was up. By the middle of the month, in exchange for life and limb the garrison had surrendered.

Source B is an extract from the *'Siege of Caerlaverock'*, a contemporary poem written to tell the story of Edward's attack.

Source B

Caerlaverock was so strong a castle that it did not fear a siege. Therefore the king came himself because it would not agree to surrender. But it was always provided with men, engines and provision for its defence…It had good woods and good ditches from side to side by water…surrounded by an arm of the sea, so that no creature could approach it on two sides without placing himself in danger…towards the south it was not easy because there was numerous dangerous ways by wood, marshes and ditches. Soon after it fortunately happened that the navy arrived with the engines and provisions. Then the foot soldiers began to march against the castle. Then might be seen the stones, arrows and crossbows flying among them. Those inside would not surrender but defended themselves that they resisted those who attacked all that day and night and the next day until their courage was considerably lowered during the attack by brother Robert who sent numerous stones from the catapult without a break from the dawn of the previous day until the evening…the Marshal and the constable, who always remained on the spot, called off the attack and they surrendered the castle to them.

To what extent do Sources A and B agree about the seige of Caerlaverock Castle? **(5 marks)**

You should compare the content overall and in detail.

Here is a weak answer:

The two sources are about the siege of Caerlaverock Castle.

Both sources agree that the Scots surrendered the castle because of English siege engines. One said, 'but once Edward's fleet arrived with his heavy siege equipment, they recognised that the game was up' and the other ones says, 'their courage was considerably lowered during the attack by brother Robert who sent numerous stones from the catapult without a break from the dawn of the previous day until the evening'.

The sources are both about the siege of Caerlaverock Castle and they both agree that it surrendered to the English.

Why is this a weak answer?

The answer is weak because:

(1) There is a very vague overall comparison.

(2) The writer does not identify what sources are being used at any time.

(3) The writer only makes one direct comparison about the use of siege engines.

Marks

- There is only one significant comparison point developed.

- At **MOST** this answer would get 2 marks out of 5, and probably only 1.

Here is a much better answer:

Overall the sources are about the Siege of Caerlaverock Castle, part of Edward I's 1300 campaign into Galloway. Both sources believe that the castle was forced to surrender because it couldn't withstand the effective English siege engines. However, they disagree in some points.

In detail, Marc Morris says the castle's chances of withstanding a siege are limited, whereas the contemporary poem disagrees by stating that they did not fear a siege. Morris's comments have the benefit of hindsight, while the writer of the poem is reflecting people's opinions of the time.

The sources disagree on the quality of the castle. Morris says that it was designed just to defend against local brigands, whereas the poem describes it as having 'good woods and good ditches from side to side by water... surrounded by an arm of the sea, so that no creature could approach it on two sides without placing himself in danger'.

Morris claims the castle defenders fought off the English knights for several days before the English fleet arrived, while the poem clearly shows that the foot soldiers and siege engines fought for several days after the arrival of the fleet before the castle surrendered.

The two sources also agree on several points. Source A states that it was the arrival of the English fleet that turned the course of the battle, and Source B agrees when it states the arrival of the navy was fortunate. Edward also had plenty of war machines. Morris says that the siege lasted only a few days in July and the poem agrees when it states that they 'defended themselves that they resisted those who attacked all that day and night and the next day'.

Finally both sources agreed that the garrison of the castle surrendered. However, Morris says that they surrendered in exchange for life and limb, whereas the poem only says they surrendered the castle to the Marshal and the constable of the English army.

Why is this a good answer?

It is a good answer because:

(1) The answer starts with an overall answer which gains 1 mark.

(2) The answer then gives at least four direct comparisons.

(3) The comparisons are relevant and connected to each other.

(4) The comparisons are identified by the author's name.

(5) Recall is used to explain attitudes or details mentioned the extracts.

(6) The answer contains comparisons of opinion but provides reasons for the differences.

Marks

This answer gains 5 marks out of 5. This answer scores highly because it follows the marking scheme process.

Now try it yourself

Source C is from the letter written by Bishop Fraser of St Andrews calling on Edward I to interfere in the succession crises.

Source C

But a sad rumour reverberated among us that our lady was dead and because of this the kingdom of Scotland is troubled and the community perplexed. When the rumour was heard and published Sir Robert Bruce who previously did not intend to come to the meeting came with a large following to confer with some who were there. We do not yet know what he intends to do or how he intends to act. But the Earls of Mar and Atholl are already collecting their army and some other nobles of the land have been persuaded to join his party. Because of this there is great fear of a general war and a large scale slaughter, unless God, through your active involvement and good offices administer justice quickly.

Source D is from Barbour's epic poem, 'The Bruce'.

Source D

For this reason, all of that party thought that the lord of Annandale, Robert Bruce ought to succeed to the kingdom. The barons were in disagreement in this and could in no way reach agreement, till eventually they agreed that their whole debate should be sent as record to Sir Edward, king of England and he should swear that without delay he would declare that decision which of these two should succeed to such an eminence. They thought this decision for the best, because at this time there was peace and quiet between England and Scotland.

> To what extent does Source C agree with Source D about
> the succession crises after the death of Margaret the Maid of Norway?
> **(5 marks)**
>
> *You should compare the content overall and in detail.*

Question Type 3 – the 'How far...' Question

This is the question that asks about a specific part of an issue and wants to find out how much you know on the subject. A useful way to start an answer to this type of question is to say '**partly**'. That gives a basic answer to the question, 'How far...'

The source will provide relevant information but will not give the whole picture. That allows you to include other information relevant to the answer from your own knowledge in order to provide a full answer.

There are two phases to any answer to this type of question:

(1) You must select relevant points from the source and develop each point with recalled detailed knowledge. There are four marks available for doing this.

(2) You must then bring in your own knowledge to show there are other points relevant to the answer that are not in the sources. This part is worth up to 7 marks.

Here is an example of a 'how far' question:

Source A is from 'The Bruce', an epic poem written by the Scottish chronicler Barbour in 1375.

Source A

The noble king and his company, probably about seven hundred, took the way towards Old Meldrum where the earl [of Buchan] and his following lay. The scouts saw them coming with banners waving in the wind and hastily went to their lord, who had his men arm themselves in haste...the king came on with great strength, and they waited making a great display...but when they saw the noble king come bravely on without hesitation, they withdrew a little and the king who well knew that they were all close to defeat, pressed on them with his banner. The lords who were still together saw that their commoners were fleeing and saw the king bravely coming, were so dismayed that they turned tail and went...when the king's company saw that they fled so disorderly, they chased them on with all their might and took some and killed others...the king was well pleased at his victory and had his men burn all of Buchan.

How far does Source A give evidence of the military abilities of Robert Bruce? **(10 marks)**

Use the source and recalled knowledge

Here is a weak answer:

The source gives quite good evidence of the military abilities of Robert Bruce. It says, 'the king came on with great strength' which shows that Robert Bruce had gained at least 700 soldiers to fight for him. The source says, 'The noble king, come bravely on without hesitation.' This shows that Robert Bruce was pressing the attack and not letting his enemies time to recover. This source tells us that King Robert was so brave that the commoners were so terrified of him that they fled. The nobles fled after their commoners abandoned them.

It says, 'When the king's company saw that they fled so disorderly, they chased them on with all their might and took some and killed others'. Which means King Robert did not allow the enemy to escape and killed many of the soldiers and took others captive. The source shows some of King Robert's military abilities, he is very brave, he pressures his enemies not allowing them time to defend themselves and he scares his enemies into running away.

Why is this a weak answer?

(1) The answer relies almost entirely on the information provided in the source.

(2) There is very little detailed recalled knowledge used to develop the points.

(3) There is no mention of any other tactics, victories or plans used by King Robert that is necessary in this sort of evaluation question. In other words the candidate ignores the 'How far' part of the question.

Marks

- The candidate only uses the source and makes the most limited development points so will only gain a maximum of 2 out of 4 marks.

- There is no recall in terms of the question to provide any balance so this candidate gets 0 marks out of 7 for this part.

Total: 2 marks out of 10.

Here is a much better answer:

The source partly gives good evidence of the military abilities of Robert Bruce. It says, 'The king came on with great strength'. Despite the losses and defeats of the previous year, Robert Bruce was still able to field a sizable army at the Battle of Siloch. The Bishop of Moray, according to Bower, had promised him 3000 fighting men, but it would appear that King Robert had only 700 available at the battle.

The source mentions several times that King Robert pressed on with the attack, allowing Buchan no time to organise his defence. This is a tactic used by Robert Bruce often. At the Battle of Bannockburn Bruce made his schiltrons more mobile and continually ordered them to advance.

Robert Bruce was also able to affect the morale of troops in a battle. His reputation was such that most commoners were too scared to fight against him and several times his Scottish enemies were forced to withdraw because of lack of support. However, he also had a positive effect on the morale of his own men. They had been worried that he was going to die of illness, but the sight of him on his horse lifted their spirits enough to fight the Battle of Siloch.

The king also knew that a 'scorched earth' policy was effective in denying his enemies important food and other resources. As well as burning Buchan, Robert also employed this tactic several times between 1314 and 1318, when his men burned villages and crops in Northern England.

We also know that Robert was personally very brave, taking part in most of the battles. His exploits at Bannockburn, especially his duel with Henry de Bohun, were inspirational to his men.

King Robert used other tactics well in his battles. He refused to fight unless the terrain was very favourable. At Bannockburn he used pits to force the knights to charge through boggy ground. Robert trained his men well. He knew that they had to be more mobile than Wallace's forces at Falkirk, he therefore learned from his own mistakes and the mistakes of others.

Overall the source gives a good impression of King Robert's military abilities but it does not give the whole picture.

Why is this a much better answer?

It is a better answer because:

(1) It selects information from the source and uses recalled knowledge to develop each point made.

(2) It provides a balance to the answer by using a lot of recall about other tactics and strategies used by King Robert.

(3) It ends with a short conclusion that shows the candidate has understood the question and thought about its meaning.

Marks

- This answer scores highly simply by following the marking scheme process.

- The candidate uses the source and develops the points well so gains 4 marks out of 4.

- There is a lot of recall and most of it is relevant. Sometimes the explanations are weak such as with Robert's invasions of England but overall this part of the answer should get at least 5 out of 7 marks, giving a total of 9 marks out of 10.

> ### Now try it yourself

Source B is an extract from the Chronicle of Walter of Guisborough.

Source B

A public robber called William Wallace, a vagrant fugitive, called all the exiles to himself and made himself almost their prince; they grew to be numerous. With him was associated also Sir William Douglas, who at the taking of the castle of Berwick had surrendered himself and his men to our king… the two Williams… thought they could find the justiciar of our king at Scone… and they hastened to destroy him. But he was forewarned and escaped with difficulty, leaving the enemy many spoils. When they had collected these, they went on no longer secretly as before but openly, confining at the point of the swords all the English whom they could find beyond the Forth and then turning to the besieging of castles.

> How adequately does Source B show the reasons why William Wallace was so important to the Scottish Resistance to Edward I? **(10 marks)**
>
> *Use the source and recalled knowledge*

> ### Question Type 4 – the 'How fully…' Question

This is the question that asks about a specific issue within the syllabus and wants to find out how much you know on the subject. A useful way to start an answer to this type of question is to say '**partly**'. That gives a basic answer to the question, 'How fully…'

The source will provide relevant information but will not give the whole picture. That allows you to include other information relevant to the answer from your own knowledge in order to provide a full answer.

There are two phases to any answer to this type of question:

(1) You must select relevant points from the source and develop each point with recalled detailed knowledge. There are 4 marks available for doing this.

(2) You must then bring in your own knowledge to show there are other points relevant to the answer that are not in the sources. This part is worth up to 7 marks.

Source A is from *Medieval Scotland*, by the historian Alan Macquarie. It talks about the importance of Bannockburn in Bruce's success in the Scottish Wars of Independence.

Source A

King Robert's triumph was complete. Thousands of English mounted knights and infantrymen had been killed, and as many captured. The spoils and booty were immense, as were the ransoms of the noble captives. The greatest prize of the day was Stirling Castle, the objective of the whole engagement; but Bruce's victory was greater than that. A really decisive battle was a rare event in medieval warfare; Bannockburn made Robert Bruce undisputed master in his own kingdom, won over the last wavering Scots (such as Alexander de Seton), and left Berwick as the only Scottish castle in English hands. The war was not over but there was little doubt left who was going to be the victor.

How fully does Source A explain reasons for the ultimate success of Bruce in maintaining Scotland's independence? **(10 marks)**

Use the source and recalled knowledge

Here is a weak answer to the question:

Bannockburn was the main reason for the ultimate success of Bruce in the Scottish Wars of Independence. It was a decisive battle, which was rare in the Middle Ages, and the English army had been decisively defeated by Bruce. He was able to capture Stirling Castle which was really important to the defence of Scotland. After Bannockburn Bruce was undisputed master of Scotland, and the Scottish nobles came over to him. Now only Berwick was left in English hands and once he recaptured it he was ultimately successful in the Wars of Independence.

Why is this a weak answer?

(1) The main weakness in this answer is that the candidate does not move away from the source. There should be a wider answer dealing with the 14 years between the Battle of Bannockburn and the Treaty of Edinburgh.

(2) The candidate only really makes the point about the Battle of Bannockburn and the advantages this brought Bruce.

(3) This part can only get a maximum of 2 marks out of 4. There is only one piece of recall that **MIGHT** gain a mark. In total, this answer would get no more than 3 marks out of 10.

Here is a better answer:

The Battle of Bannockburn was a significant factor in helping Bruce achieve his ultimate victory in the Scottish Wars of Independence. This source tells me that Bruce's triumph was complete with the destruction of the English cavalry and infantry. The battle did help Bruce capture Stirling Castle, which helped protect Scotland from future English invasions, and it helped convince the Scottish nobles who were on the sidelines to join with Bruce. The source also tells us that this was a decisive victory and made Bruce undisputed master of his kingdom.

However, it was another 14 years before Bruce achieved his ultimate success and was recognised as king of Scots by England in the Treaty of Edinburgh. In order to persuade the English, Bruce had to launch several invasions of Northern England. These raids devastated Northern England and the Scots stole a lot of wealth. Edward II tried to invade Scotland but these invasions were very expensive and failed to defeat the Scottish armies. Bruce also distracted the English from Scotland by invading Ireland in 1317 and writing several letters to the Pope in 1320 to gain his help in the struggle. The most famous of these letters was the Declaration of Arbroath and it showed that all the Scots considered Bruce to be their rightful king. Finally, problems in England helped Bruce achieve his success, as Edward II was a weak king and was eventually killed by an uprising led by his wife and Mortimer. Overall, Bannockburn was only one of the factors that allowed Bruce to achieve his ultimate victory.

Why is this a better answer?

This is a better answer but is still not perfect. The answer brings in relevant recall and shows an understanding of the ways in which Bruce achieved his ultimate victory. The whole issue cannot be covered in this answer but equally it must be understood that this question needs an overview of the main points in the issue to be successful.

Marks

This answer would only gain 2 marks out of 4 for developing the source but could gain 6 marks out of 7 for relevant recall, making a total of 8 marks out of 10.

Now try it yourself

Source B is By Michael Brown taken from his book, *The Wars of Scotland, 1214–1371.*

Source B

The oath which was sworn by John altered the status of the king of Scots both inside and outside Scotland. Even without Edward's overlordship, however, John would have faced a difficult situation.

Relatively few cases were appealed to Edward's court from Scotland, but more than any other issue, the Macduff case exposed one of the limitations of John's kingship. On his release from custody, Macduff once again complained to Edward, now John's superior lord, and the case became a test of his lordship. John was summoned to the English king's court in 1293... [John] arrived at Westminster to argue that Edward's court had no right to judge this case and he refused to answer concerning his realm without the advice of his chief men. Edward ignored this denial and threatened to charge John with contempt of court and confiscate his three chief castles. In the face of this pressure John gave in, he formally recognized Edward's authority and promise to return when the case was brought before the English parliament.

How fully does Source B illustrate the problems between King John and Edward I? (10 marks)

Timeline

Year	Date	Event
1249	13 July	Alexander III is inaugurated as King of Scots at Scone
1263	2 October	Battle of Largs
1266	2 July	Treaty of Perth
1274	19 August	Alexander III attends Edward I's coronation
		Alexander III refuses to give an oath of fealty to Edward I for Scotland but does swear for his English lands
1281	14 August	Alexander III's daughter Margaret marries Eric II of Norway
1284	29 January	Prince Alexander, Alexander III's son, dies
1285	14 October	Alexander marries Yolande, a French noblewoman
1286	19 March	Alexander III dies
	April	Guardians chosen at Scone
	November	Robert Bruce the competitor attacks castles in the south west
1290	June	Edward I seizes the Isle of Man
	18 July	Treaty of Birgham
	September	Margaret, the Maid of Norway, dies en-route to Orkney
1291	10 May	Meeting of Edward I and the Scots at Norham
	13 June	The claimants submit and give their oath to Edward I
	August	The Great Cause begins
1292	17 November	John Balliol is chosen as king of Scots
	30 November	Inauguration of King John at Scone
	26 December	King John formally swears the oath of homage to Edward I, who becomes overlord of Scotland
1293	8 February	King John's first parliament is held at Scone
1294	29 June	Edward I summons the Scots to fight in France
1295	5 July	Scots seek an alliance with the King of France
1296	March	Scots attack England
	30 March	Siege of Berwick
	27 April	Battle of Dunbar
	July	King John surrenders to Edward I
	28 August	Scots forced to sign the Ragman's Roll at the Berwick Parliament
1297	May	Wallace rebels and kills Heselrig at Lanark
	Spring/Summer	Andrew Murray rebels in the north
	June	Nobles rebel in the south west; they surrender at Irvine
	September	Wallace and Murray join up at Dundee
	11 September	Battle of Stirling Bridge
	November	Andrew Murray dies

Year	Date	Event
1298	January	Scots capture Stirling Castle
	March	Edward I returns from France
	22 July	Battle of Falkirk
1299	Autumn	Scots capture Stirling castle
1300	July–August	Edward I campaigns in the south west; he captures Caerlaverock Castle
1301	July–August	Edward I and his son campaign again in southern Scotland
	Summer	After much Papal urging, King John Balliol is released into the custody of the king of France
1302	January	Scots agree to a 9 month truce with Edward I
1303	May	The French king is forced into a treaty with Edward I. Scotland now isolated and alone
	June	Edward I launches another invasion into Scotland
1304	22 April	Edward begins bombarding Stirling Castle with his new siege engines
	20 July	Stirling Castle falls
	Summer	John Comyn and other nobles surrender to Edward I
1305	3 August	William Wallace captured
	23 August	William Wallace executed
1306	10 February	Robert Bruce murders John 'The Red' Comyn at Dumfries Abbey
	25 March	Bruce inaugurated at Scone
	19 June	Battle of Methven, near Perth
	11 August	King Robert defeated by MacDougal at Dalry
	September	King Robert flees Scotland
1307	February	King Robert returns to Carrick
	10 May	Battle of Loudon Hill
	7 July	Edward I dies at Burgh by Sands on the Solway
1308	23 May	Battle of Inverurie
	Spring	The 'Hercship of Buchan'
	Summer	King Robert campaigns in Galloway
	August	King Robert wins the Battle of the Pass of Brander
1310	September	Edward II invades Scotland
1311	Early	Edward II forced to withdraw from Scotland
1312	August	King Robert attacks northern England
1313	January	Perth captured
	February	Dumfries captured
	May	Isle of Man re-taken
1314	23–24 June	Battle of Bannockburn
	November	Parliament of Cambuskenneth
1315	May	Edward Bruce invades Ireland
	July	King Robert attacks Carlisle

Year	Date	Event
1318	1 April	Berwick captured by the Scots
	June	King Robert excommunicated and Scotland placed under an interdict
	14 October	Battle of Fochart. Edward Bruce killed
1319	Summer	Edward II besieges Berwick while Moray and Douglas invade England
1320	Early	Civil war in England between Edward II and his barons
1320	April	Declaration of Arbroath
1322	September	Edward II launches his last invasion of Scotland. Like the others, this ends in failure
	October	Battle of Old Byland – King Robert defeats the English army near Rievaulx Abbey. Edward II flees for safety
1323	30 May	13 year truce between Scotland and England
1327	20 January	Edward II deposed by Isabella and Mortimer
	Easter	King Robert leads new army to Ireland
	July–August	King Robert invades northern England
	21 September	Edward II murdered
1328	17 March	Treaty of Edinburgh at Northampton

Glossary

Archbishop A high-ranking church official who leads the bishops within his diocese and answers to the Papacy in Rome. Scotland had no archbishops during the Scottish Wars. The closest Archbishop was York; historically the Archbishop of York has attempted to exert control over the Scottish church.

Barons and baronial courts An Anglo-Norman rank of nobility. Barons swear homage to the king, promising to obey and fight for the monarch in exchange for land and the right to hold judicial courts.

Bishop A high-ranking church official who is in charge of all surrounding parishes. In Scotland during the Wars of Independence, bishops were the highest-ranking churchmen. They were allowed to make petitions to Rome without the help of Archbishops. This was something they were keen to protect.

Burgh A town that has been granted a royal charter. Burghs were allowed to trade with foreign merchants, maintain their own councils and create local by-laws.

Burgess Inhabitants of burghs.

Community of the Realm Where nobles and the leading churchmen (possibly the emerging middle classes) worked together politically for the good of the kingdom, in the absence of the king.

Chivalry/Chivalric code A set of codes and rules by which knights lived and fought. It was expected that those of the knightly orders would act in a way that reflected this code of conduct.

Earl A powerful noble ranked higher than a baron. Earls ruled over vast areas of land and could command large feudal armies.

Envoys Messengers who were empowered to speak on the behalf of those who dispatched them.

Feudalism A medieval system of government. Kings granted land (feu or fief) to their followers and in exchange they promised to fight and defend the king. In this way kings were able to gather feudal armies to fight for them.

Homage The official ceremony of accepting a grant of land from the king. Giving an oath of homage meant you were the 'man' of the king and agreed to obey him and defend him.

Inauguration The ceremony to install a king. Note that there was a legal distinction in the middle ages between an inauguration and a coronation, which required the authority of the papacy. Kings of Scots did not have the legal right to a coronation at this time

Levies Usually refers to conscripted men forced to fight in their lord's armies. In the middle ages most infantry forces were made up from feudal levies. As part of your tenancy agreement with the landowner, you were expected to fight in his armies whenever required. Some tenancy agreements included the requirement to own certain weapons or a number of horses to be used in times of war. In Scottish burghs men were expected to attend the wapinshaw, a yearly inspection to prove they had the required equipment.

Mormaers Powerful Celtic chieftains, effectively local kings. The title fell out of fashion after the rule of David I. Mormaers eventually became Scottish Earls.

Overlord A lord over other lords; a feudal superior.

Schiltron A compact formation of pikemen, usually in a circle or semi-circle, with their pikes or spears pointing outward.

Scutage Also known as shield tax, this payment was made by knights or barons who did not wish to turn up and fight for the king when called upon to do so as part of their feudal dues. The money was the equivalent of the forces they would have brought to the battle. The king then used the payment to hire mercenaries to replace the missing knight and his men.

Sheriff A royal officer in charge of local administration, taxation and calling forth feudal levies.

Sovereignty The right of a noble, usually the monarch, over the land he possesses.

Suzerainty The name given to the rule of an Overlord. He was said to have suzerainty over another domain or kingdom.

Chronicles of the Scottish Wars

Much of the information we have for this period comes from official government documents, court and exchequer rolls, letters and royal charters. While these documents provide invaluable evidence, they do leave significant gaps in the story of the Scottish Wars. To make matters worse, many of the Scottish documents prior to 1296 were lost at sea, after Edward I ordered them to be sent to England.

However, there is another group of records at our disposal which helps fill in these missing gaps in the story: the chronicles. The chronicles are records of important events, usually in chronological order, written by individuals or groups of people over a number of years. Many chronicles simply list the events year by year, and are thus called annals. However, others are either a collection of stories, or one long story or poem detailing a particular event or notable person.

There are, of course, some problems in dealing with the information found in the chronicles. Firstly, authors of the chronicles usually relied upon second-hand accounts as they were written some time after the event took place. It was common practice to re-use chronicles from an earlier age to gather information. Therefore, if one chronicler made a mistake it was quite often repeated. Chroniclers often wrote for a particular audience, which means they tended to be biased. Many are full of factual errors; some exaggerate events or statistics in order to make them more dramatic, while others rely on oral history or legends, both of which may be historically inaccurate.

Nevertheless, without the chronicles our understanding of the Scottish Wars would be severely limited. Listed here are a few of the important chronicles. Some are still available to buy today.

The Chronicle of Melrose

The authors of this are unknown but they were probably monks at Melrose Abbey. This is an important chronicle detailing major events in Scotland up to 1270. It provides a detailed account of the conflict between Scotland and Norway in 1263 and of the Treaty of Perth in 1266.

Chronicle of Walter of Guisborough

This was written in 1300 by a monk from the Yorkshire priory of Gainsborough, a religious house founded by the Bruce family. The section of the chronicle dealing with the lives of Edward I and Edward II contain many personal observations and copies of important charters issued at that time. The writer appears to be very well informed about events in Scotland in the 1290s.

The Chronicle of Lanercost

This was written in Northern England and covers the years between 1204 and 1346. It covers the events of the Scottish Wars in much detail and many of the descriptions, particularly of the Siege of Berwick and the Battle of Bannockburn, are thought to be eyewitness accounts. There is some debate as to whether the chronicle was actually written at Lanercost; some believe that it was written at Carlisle and transferred to the priory at a later date.

Vita Edwardi Secundi

This was written by a Monk of Malmesbury between 1315 and 1326. It contains a detailed account of the Battle of Bannockburn.

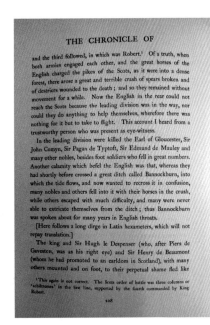

A page from the Chronicle of Lanercost

'The Bruce'

This was written by John Barbour, Archdeacon of Aberdeen. His epic poem about King Robert I was probably finished around 1375. Much of Barbour's work is based on accounts from surviving veterans and written sources that are now lost to us but some historians believe that some of the stories have been invented to increase dramatic tension. 'The Bruce' is also highly dismissive of the contributions of both King John and William Wallace, perhaps not surprising considering the audience for which it was written.

The Scalacronica

This was written by Sir Thomas Gray, an English knight who fought in the Second Scottish Wars. He was a prisoner in Edinburgh Castle for some time and wrote his account of the Wars. His father had personal experience of the first wars and fought at Bannockburn.

The Chronicle of John of Fordun

This was written in the second half of the fourteenth century. Historians believe that Fordun had access to sources that no longer exist but it is thought that he re-wrote them with a much more positive spin towards the Bruce family.

'The Wallace' or 'The Actes and Deidis of the Illustre and Vallyeant Campioun Schir William Wallace'

This was written by Blind Harry in 1488 and is believer to be heavily based on an earlier work that no longer exists. This is a rather colourful account of the life and career of William Wallace. It draws heavily on oral traditions and legends about the Scottish patriot. However, it is full of errors and historical inaccuracies. This epic poem was written at a time of increased tensions between England and Scotland and that certainly explains the strong anti-English sentiment found in the work.

The Scottichronicon

This was written by Walter Bower in the fifteenth century and is a highly important work. It relies heavily on John of Fordun's chronicle and much of the Scottichronicon was simply an expanded rehash of that work. However, there are more stories about the exploits of King Robert I, perhaps taking into account an oral record of events that now no longer survives. Bower also makes reference to other sources, such as the Chronicle of St Andrews, which no longer survive.

Bibliography

Chapter 1

Barrow, G.W.S. (1989) *Kingship and Unity: Scotland 1000–1306*, Edinburgh University Press

The Register of Dunfermline

The Acts of Parliament of Scotland, 5 February 1284

Chapter 2

Letter from William Fraser to Edward I, 1290 (National Library of Scotland, Edinburgh)

Statement by the Scots at Norham, May/June 1291 (University of Glasgow Library, Glasgow)

Chapter 3

The Chronicle of Walter of Guisborough, 1306–07

The Lanercost Chronicle, 1297

Letter from King John to Edward I, 2 July 1296 (Public Records Office, London)

Chapter 4

Letter from Hugh Cressingham to Edward I, 1297 (Public Records Office, London)

The Lanercost Chronicle, 1297

Blind Harry, 'The Wallace', 1488

Chapter 6

The Chronicle of Walter of Guisborough, 1306–07

Barbour, J. 'The Bruce', 1375

Chapter 7

Armstrong, P. (2002) *Bannockburn 1314*, Osprey Publishing

Further reading

Armstrong, P. (2003) *Stirling Bridge and Falkirk 1297–98*, Osprey Publishing

Barrow, G.W.S. (1988) *Robert Bruce*, Edinburgh University Press

Beam, A. (2008) *The Balliol Dynasty*, John Donald Publishing

Brown, M. (2004) *The Wars of Scotland 1214–1371*, Edinburgh University Press

Fisher, A. (1986) *William Wallace*, Edinburgh University Press

Lynch, M. (1991) *Scotland: A New History*, Pimlico

Macquarrie, A. (2004) *Medieval Scotland, Kingship and Nation*, Sutton Publishing

McNamee, C. (1997) *The Wars of the Bruces*, Tuckwell Press

Morris, M. (2009) *A Great and Terrible King: Edward I and the Forging of Britain*, Windmill Books

Watson, F. (2005) *Under the Hammer*, John Donald Publishers

Index